PUBLISHED BY ESTEP & FITZGERALD BOOKS

DISTRIBUTED BY INGRAM CONTENT GROUP

ISBN-10 0985857072

ISBN-13 978-0-9858570-7-3

PRINTED IN THE UNITED STATES OF AMERICA

1 0 9 8 7 6 5 4 3 2

ESTEP & FITZGERALD
BOOKS

EstepFitzgerald.com

BY DAWN WE'LL BE FREE

ONE FAMILY'S COURAGEOUS JOURNEY TO FREEDOM

Georgette Hadvina

I DEDICATE THIS BOOK TO MY BELOVED CHILDREN: EDMUND, RICHARD, AND CINDY. ALSO TO MY INCREDIBLE GRANDCHILDREN JENNA, JACK, ERIN, AND DANA, AND TO MY WONDERFUL NIECES AND NEPHEWS, ESPECIALLY STEVEN FOR ALL OF HIS GUIDANCE. THIS IS YOUR HISTORY ALSO.

"Family is where life begins and love never ends."

-Anonymous

MY OPINIONS IN THIS BOOK ARE BASED ON MY PERSPECTIVE THROUGH MY PERSONAL OBSERVATION OF THE COUNTRIES I HAVE LIVED IN. THE STORIES I TELL ARE AS I REMEMBER THEM.

GEORGETTE HADVINA

Contents

ONE

Saying Goodbye

The year was 1943. Three of us were standing on the platform at the rail station. Mama and Papa were holding each other tight. Mama was crying. She was telling Papa to watch out for this and for that and to be careful.

Papa is going far away on the train, I had been told.

I was wearing a pretty little white flowery dress, and all of a sudden the wind blew a gust of very cold air, and I got chilly. I whined about it, but Mama paid no attention to me. I pulled on her skirt until she looked down at me and smiled.

Papa picked me up, just as I heard a whistle blow close by. I knew what that meant: The train was arriving.

Papa hugged me tight.

"You know I have to go far away now," he said, sadly.

"Yes Papa, Mama told me you are going to the big, big, big city."

"Yes I am. You and Mama will come there too, when the time comes. Then we will be all together again. But for now you have to promise me," and he hugged me even tighter, "you will take care of Mama for me, won't you?"

"Yes Papa, I will..."

It was a big job for a four-year-old, but I took it very seriously.

He kissed both of us several times, and then he got up on the train. We waved until the train disappeared.

I thought back to the night before, when Mama had told me Papa was going to leave. She had been making crêpes. I loved crêpes. It was my favorite food in the whole wide world. They smelled so heavenly. They were soft, warm, and sweet. She usually made them right after supper, very fresh.

We always spent time together in the evenings. It was our special time. I sat on a chair nearby and watched her cook. She taught me poems and songs. She would give me a line or two of some poetry or song and I had to repeat it several times with the ones I learned the day before, and I would soon know a whole poem or a whole song. That was our little routine. I just remember feeling so safe in those simple times.

There was an enchanting poem, a very special one written just for me when I was born, by my mother's friend Istvan Moldvay. I only remember a few lines of it:

"When the angels were sifting snowflakes,

And the fairies were sprinkling magical moon dust."

That particular evening was very different from the usual warm and enchanting evenings I spent with my mother.

"We are moving to a big city, dear..." Mama said, with excitement.

"We *are*?" I asked.

I was happy to hear the news; I did not particularly like the flat in which we had been living. It was dark and dim most of the time and did not have a garden in which to play. My favorite thing about the place was playing in the very wide windowsills; there was a lot of light there.

We lived in an ancient city called Sibiu, which was located in Transylvania, Romania. From the windows of our flat, there was a nice view of Sibiu's main square. The ground was covered with cobblestones and there were lots of people crossing from all directions; big people, little people, and all kinds of people, some of them riding horses. The stones made a particular sound when people walked on them, especially when the horses were galloping.

Sibiu was called Szeben (in Hungarian) at the time, and was a lovely provincial city with wide boulevards, many fountains, and statues. There were beautiful parks packed full of flowerbeds, with long walking corridors under huge horse chestnut trees. The parks were used frequently, as it was customary for people to gather after church on Sunday afternoons or weekdays after dinner for a leisurely stroll. It was called korzo (the strolling place) and it was the social center of the city where people met to talk with friends and catch up on the latest news. That is where the ladies showed off their finest and newest one-of-a-kind dress creations. It was their way of enjoying a fashion show. I remember sitting for countless hours on lovely benches with my mother and her elegant friends as they discussed the importance of the length of the season's dress sleeves, according to the newest Viennese fashion.

Sibiu was a typical Austro-Hungarian Saxon city. The majority of the population was Austrian mixed with Hungarians. There were lots of clean, glistening German delicatessens, floored with white tile and full of all kinds of delicacies. Lots of fragrant cheeses were hanging from the ceilings and there were rolls and rolls of handcrafted sausages, smoked salamis, ham, and cold cuts. There were many bakeries stuffed with the finest croissants, tortes, and traditional pastries. And of course, there were the favorite watering holes: the beer gardens. These were elegant outdoor restaurants with iron tables and chairs set up under large oak trees, and were a favorite outing for my family, especially on hot summer evenings when couples danced to live bands playing wonderful melodies.

The city had theaters, concert halls, libraries, and everything that any European city offered at the time, anything a citizen wanted for fine living and an active, cultured life. According to my parents, their life was enjoyable, peaceful, and wonderful in those years.

Mama, Papa, and I, Enjoying a Peaceful Summer Afternoon at the Park in Sibiu

There was a large church on the opposite corner of the square, which had a huge clock on top of its tall tower. It was right in the view of our window, making a melodic gong sound every hour. Mama often made me count the gongs.

The windowpanes of our apartment were painted dark green and the space between the windowpanes and the frame was filled with a soft, clay-like insulator. I figured out that I could easily dig out this putty with my little fingers and roll it into a ball and even form it into a doll once I got good at it. It was a delight until my mother saw me and I had to put it all back. But now we would be moving, no more windowsills.

"Why are we moving, Mama?" I asked.

"Do you remember the man we talked to yesterday on the train?" Mama asked.

"The one who talked about the pig?"

"Yes. That is the one..." she said with sadness.

I remembered him well. He was sitting next to us on the train, well-dressed in a chocolate brown suit and reading a newspaper. He frequently looked up and smiled at me, until I started to talk with my mother in Hungarian. Suddenly, he put his newspaper down and his face turned dark and angry.

He spoke to my mother firmly in Romanian.

"Why is this child speaking Hungarian?"

"It is her mother's tongue," she snapped at him.

"I hate that pig language," he answered angrily, and he got up and walked away.

I remembered how hurt my mother's face had looked.

I didn't linger on the memory of the rude man or the fact that we were moving. I was only interested in eating the crêpes my mother had just filled with delicious apricot jam and dusted with powdered sugar. I didn't understand at the time that a huge decision had been made. A decision that would affect our destiny.

"We are moving to a big city called Budapest, where everyone speaks Hungarian and nobody calls us a pig."

At that time, Romanian and Hungarian relations were rocky. Romania had been neutral for the first two years of World War I. Then in 1916, a secret treaty had been signed: Romania would be awarded additional land if they would help fight in the war against the Austro-Hungarian Empire. This was called The Treaty of Bucharest. In 1920, The Treaty of Trianon, which ended World War I, changed many of our borders. Places that had been part of Hungary for hundreds, if not thousands of years, were now part of Romania. It was hard for people who were once living in Hungary to suddenly be living in Romania, where they were considered "pigs" to some.

I watched my mother packing for a few days and the next thing I knew, we were taking a long train ride.

When the train finally stopped, Mama said we were getting off. I remember feeling glad that our journey had finally ended. The sun was out, but a cool chilly wind hit our faces when we got down from the train.

A young woman with a round, smiley face greeted us. Her head was covered with a flowery headscarf.

"Nice to see you Miss," she said to Mama cheerfully.

"Nice to see you too, Anna," answered Mama.

I thought Anna dressed funny; she looked fat with her thickly gathered colorful skirt and an even more colorfully embroidered apron on top of it.

"My lordships are anxious to see you. They are home waiting for you," she said with excitement, taking our luggage.

"Yes, I am too. I can't wait to see them," said Mama.

Mama had explained to me on the train that we were going to live with her grandparents for a little while. She assured me I would love it, because they had a large garden that I could play in, filled with vegetables and vibrant flowers. There was a large apple orchard and lots of animals there, like chickens and ducks.

"Do they have baby ducks?" I asked.

"Well, sometimes they do," Mama laughed.

I became excited at the possibility of playing with little ducks. I loved ducks, yellow ones mostly. I thought back to how I loved the walks we used to take to the river. Mama usually sat on a bench facing the river and read a book, and I was free to play, gathering unusual rocks, and watching the sparkling water rippling and flowing. Once in a while, a duck family appeared, which was a magical moment for a child. I would usually spot the mother duck first and then several cute, yellow, fuzzy baby ducks appeared following her. They waddled from side to side, which I found humorous. I used to run after them— I wanted to catch one of them and take it home with me as my pet. Once I did manage to catch one; she was so soft and warm, but she escaped my clutches pretty quickly. Mama wouldn't allow it anyway.

When I heard there might be ducks at my great-grandparents, I thought, *Goody! Finally, I can have my own ducks!*

We climbed into an open carriage with a black canvas top. A man was sitting on the front bench holding the horse's reins.

Mama and I shared the big seat and Anna took a seat facing us.

"How is the family?" Mama asked Anna.

As the carriage rolled along, Anna told us stories of the family. She spoke in an uncommon dialect and fast manner, telling stories of all kinds of people with names that sounded funny to me.

After some time, we came to a stop. Our driver got out and opened up a huge iron gate. We had arrived.

I could see the house sitting on the top of a hill. I didn't see any flowers, let alone ducks, but there was a lot of green grass around us.

We started to approach the house and soon I could see a small, thin woman dressed in a long black skirt. She came out from the house and waved to us.

"Grandmamma!" my mother yelled. As we got closer, a man appeared also. He had snow-white hair and a large white moustache. He was wearing a black suit and a very starched white shirt with a black bow tie. He carried a silver walking cane with him. There were a lot of hugs and kisses, and somehow I knew these were my dear people, the people who would end up being my most favorite people in the entire world, the anchors in my life. I had a warm love for them for the rest of my life. My beloved great-grandparents.

My great-grandmother led us into a large dining room. In the middle of the room stood a large table surrounded by tall, dark, heavy, carved Victorian-style chairs. The table was covered with a crisp white linen tablecloth, and was properly set for lunch. All four walls were covered with crimson silk damask. A large picture was hanging on the far wall: a life-sized oil painting of a young man in his glory. Later I found out that the young man was my great-grandparents' only son, who tragically died in an accident when he was twenty-seven years old. From the dining room, where I was sitting and eating lunch, I could see the adjacent library. There were rows and rows of handsome leather books neatly arranged in the dark wood cases.

After lunch, Great-Grandfather went out to the large terrace overlooking the apple orchard and lit his pipe. He told me it was his reading time, when he caught the warmth of the afternoon sun.

Great-Grandmamma disappeared into the kitchen with Anna, and Mama and I went upstairs to the guest bedroom to unpack. Mama sat down in a large, stuffed chair in front of the window and motioned to me to sit on her lap.

"I have more good news to tell you," she said, smiling.

"I love good news! What is it, Mama? Can I see the little ducks now?" I clapped.

"No sweetheart, I am afraid you will have to wait until springtime to do that. That is when they hatch. They are all grown by now. But I have better news than that."

I was looking out the window, watching a fluffy white cloud move quickly through the blue sky. She waited until I looked at her again.

"You are going to have a little baby sibling."

THE CARPATHIAN MOUNTAINS

TWO

A Trip on the Train

"I will?" I asked. "Is it a sister sibling?"

"I do not know if it is a sister or brother as of yet. We have to wait until after the baby is born to find that out."

"Mama, I want a little sister."

"You do?"

"Yes," I insisted. "Little sisters are fun to play with."

"Well, I'll tell you what," she said, "you can name the baby if it is a girl. Do you know what you want to name her?" she asked me with a big smile.

I did not.

"Think about it. You have plenty of time."

"Is she coming soon?" I asked.

"Not that soon. In a few months," she answered.

"How long is a few months, Mama?"

"You have to sleep many, many times until the baby comes."

It was a peaceful afternoon; the room was full of the hope of wonderful experiences ahead of me.

My great-grandparents, The Rethys, were descendants of an old aristocratic Hungarian family. They were important landowners in the country; they had been living on the same land for hundreds of years. Unfortunately for them, they were in one of the Hungarian cities that had been given to Romania— and they stayed there, on the land their ancestors had lived on.

My great-grandparents lived a peaceful and provincial life on the ancient land left to them. They knew their privilege was not just about enjoying their inheritance; it came with big responsibilities. They were the custodians of the family land, and they had to be preservers. They had to uphold their inherited ancient culture, their traditions, and their way of pride. They lived a dignified life of self-sufficiency, a wonderfully prosperous and stable life.

The earth provided all of the nourishment and nurturing they could need. Their land was fertile with the promise of abundant crops. Their picturesque surroundings had a wonderful climate. East of the town was the magnificent Carpathian Mountain range, which protected them from the harsh northeast winds.

The equally-divided four seasons set the pace for a rhythm of nature and life. They were very distinct. Winters were relatively short. The snow started to fall by the beginning of December, plentiful and soft, creating an extraordinary magical beauty.

January was always a memorable month for the family, as it was the time when the land required the least amount of work, and the time when major entertainment was planned. My great-grandparents had been a popular and celebrated couple in their younger years, and were known for their hospitality and legendary parties. They had people come from all over the country for their celebrations, some of which lasted for an entire week. It was customary for their favorite guests to stay in their home that long. These wonderful events broke up the death of winter stillness.

MY GREAT-GRANDPARENTS

January was also my great-grandfather's birthday and name day. The name day was a particular European Christian ancient tradition, which started centuries ago when some Saints were designated a day to honor them. Calendars were made with every saint's name day, which was practical because people just had to look at the calendar to see to whom they needed to wish a happy name day. Parents usually chose the name of their children according to the name that appeared closest in the calendar, that way they were able to celebrate both events at the same time.

The snow usually melted by March, when the first life of earth appeared between the snow patches: little flowers with delicate white petals. The melting snow always replenished the rivers and streams with plentiful clean water. Spring was the busiest time of the year. There was a lot to do, including major cleaning and organizing.

They planted the crops, flowers, vegetables and trimmed the trees. This hard work was necessary to bring bountiful results.

Spring was when nature really came to life; their trees exploded with bountiful fragrant flowers, especially in the apple orchard. My favorite memory from those days is walking through the forest of white and pink towering trees. It was a magic wonderland for me during those balmy spring afternoons.

I was always delighted by the new generation of baby livestock that was born in the spring. These animals would provide fresh eggs, milk, butter, cheeses, and meat. I spent endless hours in the barnyard, watching the army of chickens (and of course the ducks) in every color, shape, and size. It was fascinating to watch how hard they were laboring to eat all day; they scratched the ground to find their nourishment throughout their territory. When one of them was lucky enough to catch a prized insect, the whole barnyard knew about it.

It took a while to make friends with the geese. They were the kings of the barnyard. They wouldn't let you in unless they knew you and liked you. I was bitten by a few of them more than once, but I did not give up visiting my favorite animals. Slowly but surely, they did accept me, so much so, that they started to wait for me and later they protected me from any kind of intruder.

Summer was a rewarding and fun adventure. The vegetable garden was a delight for me to play in on warm days, especially when I could harvest succulent red raspberries, gooseberries, and blueberries to my heart's desire. I was lucky they had so many bushes; nobody noticed my generous helpings of all that fresh fruit.

The dense orchard was very mysterious, with long grass and hundreds of trees growing in precise lines. They were mostly variations of apples, but there were also cherry, peach, and pear trees. It was an especially wonderful spot in which to play with my friends, and a great hiding place when Anna called me in to wash up.

Beyond the apple orchard on the top of the hill were acres and acres of land, covered by a sea of golden wheat dancing in the gentle wind. I never went far enough to see the meadows where the cows and sheep spent their days with their herders. But just before sundown, one could hear the faint symphony of the bells on their necks, which brought the promise of the creamiest fresh drink one can have. That is when I ran to the kitchen, picked up my special robin's-egg-blue mug, ran across the gardens, then across the street to have that evening's fresh nourishment. By the time I arrived there, the familiar man who milked the cows was already sitting on his three-legged stool behind one of the cows. I could see his happy smile spread ear to ear under his equally large mustache, as he watched me making my way fast as I could for my foamy, warm, delightful milk.

It wasn't just delicious farm fare that was plentiful. My great-grandmother also made sure to have an army of beautiful, mouthwatering pastries arranged elegantly on her beautiful collection of fine bone china platters. There was a wonderful and very ancient social ritual in that area of the small town. Each lady chose one afternoon of the week to have a special afternoon tea. She would have an open house to entertain whoever wanted to drop in. I remember when it was my great-grandmother's turn. Her tea tables were beautifully set and her friends came over to share a cup of fragrant tea, great pastries, and pleasant afternoon of talk and friendship. It was a delightful, elegant way to spend the late afternoon with friends. My great-grandmother always said there was no respectful household without at least seven different types of pastries on hand at all times. Somehow she and her friends kept their slender figures, most likely the benefit of that social ritual offset the damage of all that cream and sugar consumption.

Great-Grandfather Rethy was ninety years old and Great-Grandmother was seven years younger. Like most grandparents and great-grandparents, they loved to spoil their grandchildren and great-grandchildren, and they were no exception. I was a happy recipient of all of their love and affection. When I wasn't exploring the wonderful gardens, I would sit for hours on the terrace, listening to my great-grandfather's amusing stories, watching his mischievous blue eyes twinkling.

When we went for long walks to visit his friends, he always wore his black suit, starched white shirt, and bowtie. He also put on his derby-style hat and always carried his silver walking cane with him. This was 1943, but he was still dressed as a fine Victorian-era gentleman. People who saw us together always commented on how much I looked like him, which made me feel warm and happy. I loved to belong to him.

My great-grandmother was a slender, beautiful woman, even in her eighties. She was very active. She had a habit of getting up early in the mornings. I loved to spend those mornings with her, and it was my most favorite time of the day. I loved to watch her routine. First, she ceremoniously washed her face in ice-cold water; I guess that was her daily beauty routine, and it certainly worked because she did have gorgeous skin. She then grabbed her notebook. First she walked through the house and then she walked the grounds. She checked the animals thoroughly, then the gardens, making notes on what needed to be attended to that day.

Spending all of that peaceful early morning time with her, when the sun had just appeared on the horizon and the air was still crisp and fresh, was a very magical and special experience in my life.

Many generations of Anna's family had worked and helped the Rethy family by taking care of the property through the years. It was a traditional and mutually trusting relationship. Anna, who was the youngest member of her family, fed the animals, gathered the vegetables for dinner, and helped to prepare them.

The poor young woman also was responsible for me. As usually happens with spoiled grandchildren and great-grandchildren, I felt too privileged to listen to her. Thinking back, Anna was the only person in my life with whom I have ever been rebellious. I hope she forgave me for it.

I loved the preschool I attended. Every story and song was taught in three different languages. We spoke primarily Hungarian at home, but I also was taught to speak German and Romanian. Such practices were very common in that part of Europe, since all three nationalities lived together, especially in the cities.

One day, in chilly mid-November, Mama went

away somewhere. Nobody told me why she left; but soon thereafter, Anna's mother came to take me to her. "It's time for you to meet your new baby brother," she said.

"A little *brother*? No, I need a sister," I said firmly. "I had the name Ibi picked out for her, short for Violet; it cannot be a boy."

She laughed.

"Well it is a brother all right, but a very cute one. You will love him."

We walked far away, and she finally stopped in front of a building.

"Here we are," she said.

We went in, through the corridors and entered a room. There was Mama in the bed. I went over to her and she hugged me.

"Look at your baby brother," she motioned to the bassinet, which was on the other side of her bed. I went around and looked at the tiny baby, long and hard. He was all bundled up and sleeping peacefully.

"Mama, are you sure he is a boy?"

She laughed, "Yes sweetheart. Having a brother is not so bad. I have a brother, and we always played and did fun things together. Are you going to help me to take care of the baby? His name is Laszlo, but we will call him Laci."

I thought hard. *A second person I have to take care of?* But I would have done anything for my mother, so I said yes.

Months went by. Christmas came and went and there was a lot of snow on the ground.

Mama traveled a lot, and when she was absent,

Anna took care of the baby. I bossed Anna around a lot, since I felt it was my job to take care of my little brother. I somehow felt I was entitled to do so. The poor young woman worked very hard to earn her money, but she was an angel, and still managed to be very kind to me.

Whenever my mother came back from her trips, she told us stories of what she had seen.

The war is coming closer, she told us. She had seen bombed-out buildings in the nearby cities. Great-Grandpapa also talked a lot about the war with his friends. I just knew whatever war was, I did not like it.

I was five years old by that time. I had no conception that my ideal life was about to end. I would soon experience and know what war really was, more so than any small child ever should know. It would be the last time I would see my cherished great-grandparents.

It was a warm day. A lot of people were gathered around in the garden; my great-grandparents' friends, Anna and her family. There was a lot of chatter, hugging and kissing. I climbed up in the front of the carriage. Mama was holding my baby brother and there were boxes and luggage in the back. Earlier, I had watched a man ceremonially covering it all with some kind of canvas and carefully tightening up the corners. The same man got up and sat next to us as he took the reins in his hand. I looked down on my beloved people around the carriage. There were a lot of tears. I watched my distinguished great-grandfather holding my frail great-grandmother as she buried her face in a handkerchief.

Mama explained that we were going to the

railway station. I soon noticed that we were going a different way than the way we came, but I said nothing.

The sun was deep on the horizon when we stopped in front of some kind of station. A man came out, telling Mama we had to wait until late at night to cross. It was years later when she told someone our story and I realized what had really happened.

We had arrived at the new border to cross over to Hungary. If we would have went a year later, when another 100-mile portion of land was also given to Romania, we would have had to travel much longer to reach that border.

The law did not allow us, Hungarian citizens, to take any of our worldly possessions other than one little bit of luggage from our now lost country. My great-grandfather had paid a handsome bribe to the border patrol to have some of my mother's household belongings taken over the border for her new home. She had her cherished silver, hand-embroidered linens (that she and her mother so painstakingly worked on for years before she got married) and some of her oil paintings she loved so much.

The train station was at the top of a hill. As we were waiting, I watched the spectacular countryside changing colors as the sun was getting closer to the horizon. There was a green meadow down the hill, covered with green grass and colorful wild flowers. At the very far edge of the meadow was a river curving through large trees on both sides of its banks.

Past the river, there was a magnificent mountain range that changed from green to misty blue when the fog slowly enveloped it.

Above it, fluffy clouds lazily floated on the blue sky. There were three cows slowly approaching the river, munching the fresh grass. That was my last memory of the beloved country of my ancestors.

We traveled on the train for several hours. Mama explained to me that we were going to Budapest to see Papa. For the most part, I loved the train. I loved watching the vistas, finding animals, passing towns and cities;

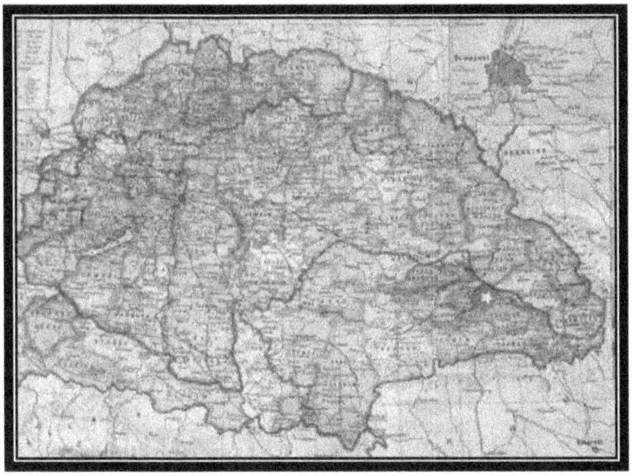

THE CHANGING BORDERS OF HUNGARY. MY GREAT-GRANDPARENTS LIVED IN THE SPOT MARKED BY A STAR

I found it interesting and entertaining. We stopped in the middle of a forest, and we stayed there for a considerably long amount of time. I was irritated. It was very boring just to sit there and look at the trees; I wanted to get on with our journey. Finally, two tall men dressed in grey came into our compartment. They told Mama that the next town was bombed the night before and it would probably be bombed again that night. They explained that it was a very dangerous situation for the train to continue, and it was decided that it would not proceed any further at that point. They said it would be safer for the passengers to spend the night on the train hidden in the woods. Hopefully we would not be noticed in the forest.

When they left, I had hundreds of questions for Mama. *Who were those men? What did they mean? Why did they come to talk to us? Why were we trying not to be noticed?* I still did not understand the concept of bombing.

I can only imagine the terror my mother must have felt that night, as she gave no sign of it to me. How frightening, to be trapped on a train with a five-year-old and a baby, in the middle of a forest.

The train did not get bombed that night and I do not remember the rest of the journey until we stopped in a very busy, noisy train station. Mama said we had arrived in Budapest and she instructed me to stay close to her at all times. She told me to look out for Papa, he was waiting for us.

We waited until most of the passengers emptied from the train, and then we finally got off. We immediately spotted Papa waiting and yelling. We were all together again, in the big city where we were going to be happy.

Little did we know our hardship was just beginning.

BUDAPEST BOMBED

THREE

War in Budapest

I later learned why we were saying goodbye to my father on a train platform.

Romania had tried to stay neutral in World War II and again, this didn't work out for them. Much of the land they had been awarded after World War I had been taken away from them again, confusing the border situation further and making people feel very disenchanted with their government. A former chief of staff had taken power— a man named Ion Victor Antonescu. He had a meeting with Hitler and when he returned, he claimed that the Reich leader had promised to return Romania's lost lands in exchange for its support of the Axis powers.

So began Romania's domination by the German war machine. Germany started to take many of Romania's exports, mainly its oil, and nothing was coming in to replace it. The economy started to go downhill. Still, Romania provided the Nazi Army with grain, equipment, and troops.

Like most Hungarians in Romania, Papa had lost his job when we lived in the flat in Sibiu, just because of his nationality. Shortly thereafter, he received a draft notice for the Army. He had no other choice but to put on his uniform and report to duty, despite the fact that he wanted nothing to do with the Nazi sympathizer army, the war, or with killing anyone. He was to report to the train station that day, with all of the other draftees. From there, the train would take them to the brutal

Russian front, where most of the fighting was occurring at the time.

My father was desperate to escape this horrible fate. As his train rolled slowly across the Ukrainian border, Father noticed that they had entered into a dense forest. The train began to pick up speed, and Papa made a split-second decision: he jumped right off that train. He was noticed right away and bullets started flying in his direction. Luckily, he was able to jump behind a large tree. The only place a bullet hit him was in his right pinkie finger. By that time, the train had gained even more speed and no one came after him. He felt his guardian angel was with him to have only his finger injured. He was not able to get medical attention for it and it healed crooked, but that crooked finger always reminded him of the brave decision that saved his life and the lives of others who he would have been forced to kill.

My father was free, but not out of trouble. He eventually hitchhiked back to Sibiu, but as a "deserter," it was very dangerous for him to stay in the flat, as he could be jailed or killed for jumping off that train and going against his draft orders. It was decided that the best option was for our family to escape Romania and move to a larger city, where we would blend into the crowds. My father had left immediately, and now my mother, brother and I followed him. We were traveling to the big, bustling city of Budapest, Hungary, where there were many places to hide.

Budapest was, and still is, one of the most beautiful cities in the world. It was once an elegant, cosmopolitan hub of Europe, home to a magnificent and cultured life. There were refined clubs, remarkable restaurants, and charming coffee houses. The majority of the city's buildings were neo-classical in style. The exquisite architecture told the tale of a rich, historical past. Budapest had shared many of the architects who designed and built Paris in the late eighteenth century.

The city had been built at the bank of one of Europe's major rivers, the Danube, and it was actually two cities combined. Buda, the smaller part of the city and also the oldest, was located on the west side of the river. It was nestled in between many hills, which provided a superb view to the Danube. There were remaining fragments of a two-thousand-year old Roman settlement, Pannonia, and the glittering thermal baths of the Gellért. There were still many old stone-studded Roman roads and fragmented stone walls through the older sections of the city, which gave the place an impressive and monumental feel.

Pest was newer. This part of the city sat on the east side of the river and was larger than Buda. Because of its flat geography, it was able to spread out further. Pest was the cultural center of the city, with graceful and statuesque churches, a marvelous grand opera house, captivating museums, a golden baroque comedy theater, and concert halls full of music. The crown jewel of the city was the grand and illustrious gothic architecture of the huge Parliament building overlooking the river. It was the fruit of labor of many generations, who had invested their hard work so the beautiful building could be used and enjoyed by all.

Before World War II, the city was prosperous and bustling with commerce. Shops filled with grand clothing, enterprising offices, and brimming factories were the sign of its successful industrial age. But the war had wrought massive damage on the city. The opulent palace of Buda, which once sat on the hill overlooking the Parliament building, was now simply a flat pile of bombed-out rubble. Many of the formerly-beautiful buildings, shops, and churches had been transformed into half-destroyed shells. Under the grinding weight of war, the city had become weary, grey, and shabby; just a shadow of her past splendor.

My father had arrived alone in this strange city, and had rented a large sunroom from an old lady who lived in the eastern suburbs of Pest. He lived very frugally, saving every penny for furniture so his family could start a new life.

When I arrived with my mother in Budapest, I remember walking into the room and looking at its large windows. It was in a suburb, on a road mostly used for walking. Only the occasional car came by. Papa very proudly showed us his newly-purchased furniture, a homecoming gift for my mother. It was a set of very fine, carved bedroom furniture, made of walnut wood. There were two armoires, two twin beds, a dressing table, and some night stands. They certainly were splendid, richly adorned with fine European master carvings of grape leaves and grapes. They were just fancy enough to be tasteful without being overdone.

My father had purchased a pretty, white bed for me. It was positioned next to the window, where I had a superb view of a garden and part of the neighborhood. A large billboard was very visible from my bed, advertising fine tea biscuits. It pictured a very cute little girl with Shirley Temple curls sitting on the floor, munching delightfully on some biscuits from a big box in front of her. That billboard haunted me for many years to come on days where I was ravenously hungry and wishing I could eat some of those biscuits.

We moved to a large apartment house a short while later, occupying a corner unit, which had a view of a railroad track from one of its window banks. Occasionally we would see a train and passengers coming by. The opposite side of the apartment overlooked a park. Part of it was built for children's delight and had swings, a merry-go-round and slides. It was fun to look out the window and watch all of those activities.

Our breakfasts were wonderful. First we took a short walk to the neighborhood bakery, which had a wonderful, tantalizing smell of freshly baked bread. I knew when I smelled that wonderful aroma that I would soon be consuming bread with fresh butter and a fruit jam. After our afternoon naps, we went to the park to play, swing, and make friends. Life was wonderful. I enjoyed every day.

I had no clue what was waiting for me.

It happened one night, out of nowhere, right after supper. The evening started out just like any other ordinary night. I watched my mother set the table ceremoniously, as she always did, even for a simple dinner. She made sure everything on the table was just right. It was part of a ritual that proper etiquette dictated; it was handed down to her by her mother and grandmother, who learned it from the generations before them.

Suddenly, the peaceful quiet night was broken by the sound of horrifying warning sirens; they got louder and louder. I didn't know what they meant; I didn't know they were warning us that planes stuffed with bombs were headed our way, attempting to bring destruction and death. My parents' panicked expressions signaled that something was not right. Seeing my mother so frightened brought me physical pain, and tears sprang to my eyes as the noise became more intense.

Just as I climbed down from my chair, my father's towering figure appeared at the door, he said something to us that I couldn't make out, the only thing I heard was, "Quick!"

Mama went to the windows and jerked the heavy curtains tightly together. I ran to her as she was doing so and she pushed me aside as she ran to the second window. I quickly went after her, clinging to her skirts, but she brushed me aside as she swiftly closed the other curtains and ran to my baby brother's crib. By then he had woken up screaming, rivaling the sound of the sirens.

Papa ran into the bedroom and came back out with coats and blankets on his arm, just in time: as soon as he reappeared in the living room, the electricity was shut off and the room went dark. He flicked the lighter he always carried in his pocket and lit a very small alcohol lamp in the corner. I was clinging hard on mama's leg, desperately needing comfort, but she was trying to quiet the baby. Papa quickly put a sweater on me, and Mama bundled up my baby brother. They made it very clear to me that we had to run.

What is going on? Why do we have to run?

I knew something of a serious and petrifying nature was happening.

We ran out to the dark corridor to an equally dark staircase. At the bottom of the wide concrete and iron steps, there were a few people holding dim lights; we could see their long shadows on the wall. “Quick, quick!” my father urged as he tried to maneuver the blankets and the lamp down several sets of stairs. By then, many of our neighbors living in the building were running with us. We finally came to the large steel door of the bunker basement. The door opened to more stairs that were much steeper and narrower. Suddenly the air was cold and I smelled a musty odor mixed with the smell of vinegar.

The staircase led into a large, dark, unfinished concrete room with all kinds of equipment in it. There were many bunk beds lined up in rows like soldiers' barracks. People started to occupy them fast, so we went and sat on some beds right in the middle of the room to mark them as ours. People were moving nervously and everybody was talking at once, trying to position themselves on the beds.

A man shouted out loud, "Be quiet and listen!"

Faintly we could hear the deep sound of heavy engines in the distance.

A few minutes later, someone said, "Here they come!"

I wondered, *Who? Who is coming?*

The deep roar became louder and louder as the bomber planes approached us. Then I heard one of the loudest, most terrifying sounds I had ever heard in my short life— it was the sound of at least a dozen roaring planes, getting louder and louder, closer and closer. All of a sudden we heard *massive* explosions, and those got louder and closer as well. Soon the sound of the bomber planes was right over our heads and we heard them spraying their deadly gifts over our city, over our homes. With each explosion, the dark building shook with the force of an earthquake. Our dim, emergency oil lamps swung violently from their hangings on the ceiling. I was shaking, absolutely trembling in terror. I was clinging tightly to my father's broad chest as he tried to cover my ears, but it was impossible not to hear the deafening roar.

Women started screaming; some prayed out loud.

God help us!

It felt like an eternity, but the planes finally passed and the noise grew less and less until we no longer heard it.

"We made it," someone said.

"How do you know?" asked another person.

"We don't. It is better to spend the night here,"

BUDAPEST DESTROYED

said a woman in the next bunk.

"The 'all clear' siren has not sounded yet."

I was really tremoring by that point, but I did not cry or whine. I knew that the adults around me were deeply frightened. I wanted to ask my mother what was going on, but seeing her anguished face, I knew it was not the time for it. We spent the night in that bunker. I am sure people went out to investigate the damage and see if the coast was clear, but since I was a child, I was sheltered and unaware of the actual destruction until the following weeks and months.

From then on, the sirens were a regular occurrence. They could come at any time, day or night. Sometimes they sounded daily; sometimes we had a week of peace. It was the beginning of extreme horror, a nightmare that surrounded us for many months to come. I could never get used to the sound of sirens signaling the coming explosions, the possibility of death. Everything that was "normal" completely ceased to exist. Our lives would never be the same; we would never be able to turn back to the days of a peaceful existence. We never knew what the next day would bring, or if we would be dead in the morning.

BOMBS DROPPED ON BUDAPEST

It could happen at any time. Our nervous systems never got used to that kind of mental torture, but we continued to live, overwhelmed with fear.

Going down to my beloved park was now forbidden; it was deserted. Swings slightly moved in the wind sometimes, but there were no longer children occupying them. There was no laughter. There was no playing. There was only terror.

My mother tried to explain it to me one day.

"If the siren comes when we are in the park, we would not have enough time to run to the bunkers and we could be in danger," she said. But now I see she meant "blown up." It was too big of a risk to go to the park. Everyone stayed close to the bunkers, afraid for their lives.

The Nazis were taking over Europe country by country. The strength and the viciousness of Hitler's well-designed, strong army was so superbly skilled, that the western part of Europe was engulfed quickly. Holland, Belgium, and France were taken over mostly by surprise, and without much resistance.

The same thing happened on the Eastern front: Austria, Poland, Czechoslovakia, and Hungary were next. Nazism was spreading rapidly, like out-of-control cancer cells. One man had a big agenda to rule the world, and it appeared he was going to have his way.

I asked my mother when I was a little older, what the initial attraction of Hitler was. How was it that millions of seemingly intelligent humans had democratically elected and followed such a person?

She remembered his speeches. In the beginning, he had painted the future of Europe under his direction as a wonderful utopia. *Deutschland überall* was his mantra. He promised he would build Germany to be the richest, most advanced country in the world. People thought that sounded like a great idea.

Like many of history's notorious dictators, Hitler had a way of getting the people to trust him. Once in power, he quickly, but surely, built a secret network of loyal and well-paid men to control the masses. No average German citizen could have foreseen what was coming. Like many socialist, fascist leaders, Hitler had to find a villain to blame for peoples' trouble and like many dictators before him, he chose to blame the rich.

He started to attack them first. Most of the banks and factories were in the very capable hands of highly-educated, smart and wealthy Jewish businessmen. They were Hitler's first order of business, and his henchmen went about removing them. Nobody believed what was about to happen *could* happen, especially the Jews.

Mama remembered that many of her Jewish friends were suspicious of Hitler from the beginning. They didn't buy his vicious speeches or fall for his words and they didn't think their fellow citizens should trust him. Regardless, none of them thought a country could be changed and reorganized that rapidly and efficiently. No one thought a ruler with a sinister and power-hungry agenda could so quickly control and destroy the lives of millions.

Before we knew it, German troops were deporting over 400,000 Hungarian Jews to concentration camps in Germany and Poland. Ninety percent of them were immediately put to death. One in three Jewish people killed in Auschwitz was a Hungarian citizen.

Mama told so many stories of how the poor Jewish people first had to live with different methods of humiliation, and later they had to face the pure vicious horror of Nazi concentration camps. She said not one of the women in her Jewish circle of friends ever dreamed the Nazis would go as far to as to kill them.

For the first few months, the Jewish people were made to wear a yellow star on their clothes, and then it progressed to things like only being allowed to shop on certain days. My mother despised the unfair and unjust policies. Her way of protesting was to go shopping for her Jewish friends who needed things. She was fully aware of the danger of her actions, but continued to do it.

During this time, the Soviet Army was also trying to oust the Nazis from Hungary. We didn't know what was worse. I was still only five years old during those big battles, and I remember them vividly. It was an unforgettable, dreadful experience that will stay with me for the rest of my life. Especially the sounds. They were the most frightening. The sirens, the bomber planes approaching, the explosions, the people's anguish and crying. Nothing is more frightening to a little child than seeing the grown-ups, the people "in charge," being frightened out of their wits. We only lived a couple of miles from the main airport of Budapest, so we were right in the middle of the most intense bombing the area had to endure.

We soon learned the Communists were just as vicious as the Nazis. Nearly 40,000 Hungarian civilians were killed during their siege, either from violence, or from starvation or disease.

Like a lot of things in life, sometimes one can become conditioned to even the most ghastly of things. My routine became hearing sirens, going into bunkers, waiting for bombing to be over and going back home. Death and destruction was my reality at the time. I remember seeing a severed human leg in the rubble on the street. My mother pulled me away, but it was too late.

Christmas came during all of this. I remember we had a Christmas tree with a single gift underneath, a doll for me. I have no idea how my parents got a Christmas tree in the midst of the war, or a doll for that matter. It must have been a lot of effort on their part to make that atrocious time as normal as possible for us children, to keep the magic of Christmas for us.

One day, shortly after Christmas, my mother's friend Tuczy arrived at our apartment, sobbing hysterically. Her parents lived in one of the smaller towns, out in the country. On Christmas Eve, they were sitting down to dinner in their beautifully decorated home. The soup had just been poured when the sirens went off. They had to flee to the nearest bunker, which was far, in their case.

The bunkers were supposed to be safe-havens, the one thing people could generally count on to protect them from bombings. But not this bunker on Christmas Eve. A bomb hit it and none of the occupants survived. Tuczy went to her parents' home to check on them and the soup was still in the bowls, the table was still set, the house was still decorated for Christmas. But her parents were no longer alive.

My mother had grown up with Tuczy and her parents, so this was a huge blow to her as well. She had spent many pleasant, memorable years with them. I also think it shook her to realize that the bunkers were not a guarantee of safety. There was no true safety at all. No place was safe from the intrusion and violence of the clashing armies.

One day, there was a knock at the front door. Papa was not home, so my mother, thinking that it must be a neighbor, went to answer it. I followed her to the door, and peeked around her skirt as the door swung open. My heart stopped when I looked up and saw a young German soldier standing there.

Budapest during the fight between the Germans and the Russians

FOUR

The Soldiers

I saw the look on my mother's face. She was absolutely petrified.

Will he rob us? Shoot us? Will this be the end? I held my breath.

The soldier stood there as we prepared ourselves for the worst. But he was not an evil man. Surprisingly, he was one of the few kind souls.

He gently said, "I know you have young children. I just want to warn you, we are going to blow up the adjacent railway in half an hour. Maybe it would be safer for you to take the children out farther away."

My mother couldn't believe it. She thanked him, closed the door, and dressed us quickly.

We were out the door as fast as we could go. We had walked about two blocks away when we heard a massive explosion. Just then, Papa came running up behind us and grabbed us, hugging us. He had returned home and we weren't there— someone in the street had told him that we were heading the opposite way.

We had survived another day.

The dust from the explosion settled and the adjacent road was suddenly filled with a Russian convoy of at least twenty military trucks.

With lots of caution, we slowly went back to the apartment. Papa went in first, and then when he motioned for us, we followed him. The sight was unbelievable. All of our windows were blown out and shattered. The wind was blowing whatever was left of the torn draperies. Glass and debris were all over the floor.

"What are we going to do?" asked Mama. I could see she was frightened. "We can't stay here."

"No, we can't," said Papa as he took the broom and started to sweep the floors.

ONCE BEAUTIFUL BUILDINGS

Mama started to cry.

Papa hugged and comforted her.

“It could have been worse,” he said.

“That’s not it,” she said. “I am just thinking that sometimes you find kindness from the most unexpected sources. If the German soldier had not warned us, I...I...I don’t even want to think about it.”

Little children learn in peculiar ways. It is not always what they have been taught with words, it is sometimes by observation. The German soldier’s compassion that day stayed with me for a lifetime. I always wondered what happened to him.

My mother asked my father again what we were going to do— there was no way we could stay in the apartment with the windows blown out and glass everywhere.

"I will think of something," Papa said. "We can spend the night in the bunker."

We started to pack some of our belongings, when there was another knock on our door.

We froze.

Who could this be?

A neighbor had come by. She looked around sympathetically, telling us her place was also blown out. She told us that no one could use our assigned bunker anymore— there was a Russian soldier occupying it.

I saw my father's face change. He looked concerned.

Then he thought of something. He said he had a former colleague, who lived only a few blocks away in a tiny house. He had been a kind man, maybe he would help us out until we found a place to live.

We had no other choice; we walked to his house and hoped he would let us stay there. By the time we got there, it was dark. The man and his wife were eating dinner; I could smell the bean soup. They were kind and understanding. Although their place was very little, they were more than happy to have us stay there. They offered us dinner but my parents refused it of course, as they knew how valuable and scarce food was.

Papa went back to the apartment and got some blankets, and we all slept on their dining room floor.

A few days later, Papa found a house for rent. We were told it had belonged to a very old

Jewish lady, who had been taken to one of the concentration camps, unfortunately. Some of her friends had arranged to rent out her property.

The house was lovely. It had large windows overlooking a beautiful garden, which was in her spring glory, despite all the destruction around her. There were stunning purple lilac trees, and packs of colorful tulips blooming. Some of the windows were inlaid with crystals. It was magic when the sun shone through the windows; there were a million beams of color dancing around the room.

No sooner had we settled into the new house, when we were caught off guard by hard knocking at the door. Through the thin glass insert, we clearly saw there were four Russian soldiers standing at the door.

This had to be it. We couldn't be that lucky twice in a row.

Papa motioned to us and whispered, *Go quickly, go to the bedroom and be quiet.*

We had heard a lot of rumors about Russian soldiers' brutality. We were frozen with fear, hoping they wouldn't shoot Papa or come in and terrorize us. He spoke with them for a long time, and then we heard the door closing. Papa came into the bedroom with a smile on his face.

"That was close," he sighed with relief.

"What happened?" asked Mama. "What did they want?"

"They are moving into the house next door. They are going to use it as their headquarters. One was a captain, and he wanted to know if I would do some work on the house for them. I said I would." He was no fool.

They were also looking for liquor, and wanted to know if we had any. We did not, but we did have a couple of alcohol lamps, which they promptly took, along with the refill bottles. Papa wondered aloud if they going to use it or drink it.

With all of the constant panic and conflicts around us, sometimes a person had to stop and give some sliver of gratitude, especially if any of the people we considered our enemies had some goodness in them.

In the case of our new neighbors, we were again lucky. The Russian captain turned out to be a very decent man, and he told his soldiers to protect us. Papa rebuilt closets and shelving for them in their headquarters, and they paid him with cigarettes, but also with railroad passes, which came in very handy within the next few weeks. I was able to play in the garden, which, to my delight, was adorned with many garden statues. They were my playing partners.

We learned that the house they were using belonged to one of our country's famous fiction writers, Erdős Renée. She had built it for one of her relatives. Both Erdős and her family had been taken to one of the concentration camps. I later read that she was one of the lucky ones who was able to survive the atrocities.

A few months later, however, the Russians abandoned their new headquarters. The captain came over and said goodbye. As he was leaving, he told us how very happy he was to be able to return to his home and to his family. He said he couldn't wait to see his children who were so similar to my brother and me.

After he left, Papa said, “He must love his children very much.”

He said we were lucky that we children reminded him of his own. That must have been the reason he had treated us reasonably well.

With the soldiers gone, we felt a little less scared. The actual fighting of the war had ended; we were no longer occupied by Nazis. There were jubilant gatherings all through the city. Clean-up started, but food was still utterly scarce, as all of the neighborhood markets were empty. Somebody told us that a central market close to the Danube had some food available, so we immediately went.

I remember the day we took the torturous journey with streetcars and buses to get there. There were many hundreds of burned, bombed-out buildings everywhere, street after street, everywhere we looked. The sights will be etched in my memory forever. The roads were full of rubble, so sometimes the bus had to wait for a long time for the opposite traffic to stop, so it could continue safely. Finally, we got to the Danube River and I saw a sight I would never forget. All of the bridges were bombed to pieces. There were just some twisted iron bars sticking out from the river. Destruction was everywhere we looked. The marks of vicious battles were everywhere.

We stood in line for what seemed like ages. When we finally entered the store, it was nearly barren. But Mama managed to purchase some carrots and some powdered milk.

The food shortage became dangerously critical. People from the city had to travel down deep into the country to get food straight from the farmers. Lack of money was our biggest issue. Papa had found work in a factory that had somehow survived the bombings, but we were still very poor from the long months of the war. He had not been able to go to work on many days.

Somehow God still provided for us. Someone told Papa about a village farmer who was willing to trade items for food. Papa had some leftover railroad passes from the Russian soldiers. He put those in a bag, along with some silver, some of my mother's jewelry, sweaters, and some of my toys, even the beautiful doll I got for Christmas.

He left and we sat there praying for his safe return. Would he be able to bring food? Would he make it back from the village?

When he finally got back, he brought some salt

and lots of oatmeal. He also had corn, flour, sugar, and beans. Mama was delighted; now she could at least feed her kids for a while, especially her toddler. One day my grandmother, my mother's mother, came to live with us. She was going blind from an inoperable brain tumor that was putting pressure on her optical nerves. She was having a hard time taking care of herself.

We were a little cramped in the home we were renting, but we were together as a family, and life was relatively pleasant. Until the sweet old Jewish lady who owned the home showed up one day on the doorstep. She had survived the concentration camp. She wanted to claim her home back, and we didn't blame her.

Now what? We were soon to be homeless. It was a disaster. There were practically no available homes left in the city.

My mother as a toddler with my grandmother, circa 1912

Everything had been taken, and thousands of once-habitable places had been destroyed by bombs.

My mother had a cousin who lived in a little town in a suburb of the Buda side of the city. He was married to a dashing Austrian woman. One of her relatives had decided to move back to Austria to take care of a needy family member and they were looking for trustworthy people to temporarily rent their house until they could return. We were delighted at this good fortune. My parents made a deal with her relative, a lease with an option to purchase the home. It was stipulated that if the owners decided never to return, we would buy the house. But in the meantime it was a lease, with the agreement to vacate the house immediately upon their return. It was a perfect short time solution; we had someplace to live, at least for the time being.

The house was a little small for the five of us. There was a small day room in the middle of the house that served as both our cramped living and dining room. Adjacent to the day room were two doors that opened into two bedrooms. My brother and I shared a room with our grandmother. The house had a large, lovely, country kitchen with brick floors and an oversized pantry. You could see it was built with a lot of thought, love, and style. Tall, narrow French windows were adorned with beautiful green-painted shutters. The front door had pretty, decorative frosted glass inserts in a delicate, classic design. The front porch was the most stylish part of the house; it was spacious with Greek-style double pillars and elegant spindles.

The view from the home was pleasant and very

peaceful. It overlooked a series of gardens and fruit tree orchards. There were also a few brilliant rose gardens. Everything grew happily in the rich soil. It was truly a wonderful little paradise. It had clearly been loved and well-tended. That garden really became our savior. It gave us the gifts of abundant fruit, vegetables and herbs that saved us from starvation in the coming years.

Far away, the horizon was lined with beautiful rolling hills and mountains whose tops melted into the cool blue sky. The best part of the property was that it was very private, quiet, and peaceful. The home did not have central heating or plumbing, but regardless, we were just happy to have someplace to live and felt lucky.

I found my mother crying one day as she unpacked her favorite possessions. She was thinking about what had happened to us. The borders had changed on our country and suddenly we were foreigners, in another country that didn't like us. It was madness. It had been so crazy and so unfair. We had been forced to leave our home, forced to smuggle our own possessions. She just couldn't wrap her head around it sometimes; it was so unjustifiable, so cruel. All of these frightful and ridiculous things had happened for bizarre political reasons.

With all that hardship and tragedy behind us, we had a lot for which to be thankful. Slowly the stores were filling with a little more merchandise, and things started to look up slightly. We were honestly just happy to be alive, be with our family, have a place to live, and have enough food not to starve.

My parents' lovely bedroom set fit perfectly in

the new house and it was a miracle that most of our furniture had stayed intact, despite the bombings. Mama had great taste in decorating; she painted the walls in very pleasant pale greens. She was very happy that she was finally able to frame and hang all of her beloved art that she and her family had collected for many years. In the dining room, she hung four original oil paintings of lovely still-life fruits. My favorite one was a painting of a bowl of oranges; they were so exotic to me. I had never seen or tasted oranges or bananas in all of those years growing up. The regal paintings were my only reference to them.

THE SOVIET ARMY

FIVE

Nazis Out, Soviets In

Slowly, the Soviet army took over Hungary and began to occupy it. In the beginning, when Communism started in our city, my father was idealistic. He was full of hope for a good life. He gave it a chance. He thought maybe it would work; maybe things would be better.

The Soviet Army created a government for Hungary in 1945 and appointed a Communist Hungarian named Mátyás Rákosi as General Secretary of the Hungarian Communist Party. He was completely aligned with Soviet Russian politics, describing himself as "Stalin's best Hungarian disciple."

This government was supposed to be in place until an election could be organized for us. They made it look like they were letting us be, but they had really only retreated to some remote places in the country.

Our new government held its first election, and our political leaders were full of enthusiasm and lots of promises for us citizens. The election was a joke— there was only one party running and it received 98 to 100% of the votes. It was clearly designed to make us feel that we had a democracy, which was in no way going to be the case.

There were speeches made about how well the Communist system worked. They successfully impressed upon the minds of many people, especially the young, idealistic ones. They promised a utopia for the masses. Their main mantra was that we would collectively own all of the factories, banks, retail stores, and farms. People liked the idea of sharing all of those promised profits. So many people had had their property destroyed or damaged, and the economy was non-existent. Working less and earning more? It was exactly what a beaten, tired and poor country wanted. Hungary was to be a Promised Land, a Garden of Eden, The "Workers' Paradise"...

Immediately, a five-year-plan was drawn out. The first thing on the agenda was to "nationalize" all of the big farms, banks and factories. The farms were taken from their owners and made to be collectives. The idea was to pull together all of the country's resources and work as a collective entity. We were all to share in these harvests; we were all to share in the profits. We would finally have food! And money!

Shortly thereafter, all of the other types of private properties were nationalized. First the apartment buildings. Then the offices and retail stores. And last of all? The private homes.

Suddenly, our rented house became the property of the state. We also lost the right to exercise our option to purchase the home. After "assessing" us, the government allowed us to stay in the house as renters and pay our rent directly to them. We had no other property rights.

Other people had it worse. Many people lost all of their rights to their own family homes. But the law of the land was firm and it was clear: there was no longer such a thing as private property ownership or private property rights. No property could be bought or sold privately. Period.

The renters had no rights to sublet their places and could not move freely. If a citizen really had to move for any reason, the only way it was permitted was for that person to find somebody who was willing to trade habitations — and even *that* had to be approved. Because of this, travel and migration were almost impossible. Since we were just renters, it did not make much difference to us. We thought we might even have stability in our situation.

Another thing on government's agenda was to eliminate the existing Hungarian currency, called pengő. I clearly remember how, in those days, we used to wait for Papa at the railroad station when he brought home his weekly pay. We would run as fast as we could to the nearest market before they closed because we needed to buy groceries, and day by day, the inflation was getting steeper. One day we could buy groceries, and the very next day all we could afford was one thing. My mother used to say that we could barely afford a book of matches with Papa's weekly salary. By that point, it took millions of pengős to buy anything. Then they started to issue special stamps on the money. I remember a storekeeper asking for two pink ones with a green stamp on them. I didn't know it then, but Hungary was experiencing the highest hyperinflation ever recorded, and the Soviets' solution to stabilizing the economy was to get rid of the pengő and bring in new currency. The next thing we knew, everyone was throwing away their useless pengős (I got to play with them) and the forint became the new currency of Hungary.

Papa still worked as an inspector in the large manufacturing plant. Mama went to work as a preschool teacher. I was sad she took a job, but

I guessed it had become very hard to feed a family of five with only Papa's salary. But that wasn't the only reason she returned to work. At first, the government had "strongly urged" all women to work; later, it became obligatory. Since equality was preached, women were expected to do all kinds of jobs, even men's jobs, like driving combines and working in factories.

We had no television available to us at the time, so the government reached the citizens with mandatory town meetings, radio messages on government-owned stations and lengthy government films shown before every approved movie. It was always the same message: How well Communism worked. We saw images of women being praised for excellent work while dressed in men's overalls, pouring hot iron or assembling machinery. The main idea was that every person had an obligation to work hard in order to provide collective benefit to all.

Poor Mama had a hard time working six days a week. She came home in the evenings and had to attend to us children, her mother (whose eye sight got worse), and the house. She did not have the conveniences of a dishwasher, a washing machine or a vacuum, and she sometimes had to chop wood for the fire before starting dinner.

Food was scarce, despite the garden. There was rarely milk, meat, or eggs in the markets. We purchased a few live chickens to supplement our diet with some eggs. All of the food staples were rationed: flour, sugar, and cooking oil. Rice, black pepper or other kinds of imported foods were just simply not available. We could only buy what the government allowed us to buy. Once a month, a coupon arrived in the mail in the form of stamps, with a certain minimum amount per person. That was the only way we were able to buy our basic food, if we were lucky to find it in the stores. As soon as any item came in, a long line instantly formed. If you were one of the unlucky people at the end of the line, there was a chance the store would run out of the product, and you had to wait until the next shipment, which could take weeks.

The entire intent of Communism was that the country's profit would be divided equally among the workers. And again, this completely failed because it was impossible for one entity to know what amount to produce, and what price to set to make a profit, so the result was that there was no profit to be divided. The planning of production was not efficient; the actual production did not even come close to sustaining itself. They weren't watching the bottom line, so the opposite ended up happening: the cost of manufacturing an item was more than the profit that item would generate, so production was slow and ridiculously inefficient. Whatever small amount of goods even available was so expensive that no one could afford it. So much for a Communist paradise.

That wasn't all. New changes were on the horizon.

60f
RÁKOSI MÁTYÁS KULTURHÁZ
BUDAPEST
MAGYAR POSTA

SIX

Property of the State

Shortly after we moved into the new house, I had started the second grade. The neighborhood school was run by the Catholic Church at that time and the teachers were mostly nuns. By the end of the first semester, I noticed that the nuns started to become very agitated— and rightfully so. The Communists were ready to take over the school system.

Mátyás Rákosi, the Hungarian leader appointed by the Communists in 1945, had initially been willing to work with people, but by 1947 things had changed. People were now starting to truly be pressured to submit to Communism. The Communists now had complete control, and they stopped pretending that any of us had a say. Rákosi finally gave people a choice: cooperate or face the consequences. No more pretending that this was a democracy.

One of Rakosi's goals for the new Communist Hungary was to overhaul the school system, especially the religious ones.

The church was one of the enemies of socialism, since they were convinced it was a strictly materialistic ideology. I remember one of the nuns brought in a radio to school, and had us listen to the important trial of the leader of our Catholic Church, Cardinal József Mindszenty.

The Cardinal was very outspoken for the people. He thought they should have freedom of religion in our country. Freedom was, of course, one thing Communists did not practice or understand. The trial went on and on for months. The issue was more than just one man's ideology clashing with the government's policies. The real issue was how the outcome of that trial would impact all of our personal religious rights and freedom.

JÓZSEF MINDSZENTY

The Cardinal was tortured into confessing all sorts of things he did not do. Shortly before he was arrested, he wrote a letter saying he hadn't been involved in any sort of conspiracy toward the government, etc., and any confessions made by him after his arrest were under duress. Lo and behold, they tortured him into "confessing" that he had organized the theft of the country's crown jewels, and that he had planned a third world war, among other ridiculous things.

After the Cardinal's imprisonment, just like everything else, the churches became property of the state. All religious schools and hospitals were nationalized. The actual churches stayed intact and state-selected priests were allowed to preach. But even though the churches were still standing, anyone who entered them was watched, and noted. It was looked upon as very risky business to go into a church and worship. Anything that wasn't Communist was done away with, and if you didn't go along, you were arrested for treason or worse. The nuns were facing a bleak future. As the nationalization of schools became the reality, they automatically lost their jobs.

The state declared them unsuitable to teach the future generation. They were labeled as enemies of the people. What happened to them I do not know. I heard they were relocated with all of the other intellectual enemies in some remote part of the country. They were forced to do some kind of manual farm work.

New teachers were hired and school life changed. The new teachers had an objective besides the common school subjects. We children now had to learn the Communist dogma or, more accurately, be forced to become enthusiastic little pioneers of the new religion of the state: Stalinism.

It was considered our obligation to worship our

wonderful, all-knowing, dear leader, Stalin. It was emphasized that we must take it very seriously.

The doctrine of Communism came very fast and very hard. We learned all of the evils of Capitalism, especially the evil idea of profit-making and how the business owners took advantage of the working class. We were made to watch endless hours of propaganda films about collectivism, and the achievements of state-owned factories; the excellent production methods the central planning bureau had created. Their major message was always that the promise of utopian society could be achieved if every person became dedicated to hard work and production. Because of the great emphasis on equality for women, we girls were taught that it was our duty and obligation to work as hard as possible to benefit our society.

We were to share the fruit of our talents and hard work with the entire population.

The government did everything in their power to "equalize" us in the classroom. It was not an easy task under the circumstances. Most of the students were much too poor to be able to afford uniforms for every day, but we all had to wear some kind of white top and our red pioneer necktie, showing proof to the world of our just and perfectly equal system.

Class warfare was thought about every single day. How the bourgeoisie were using the poor proletariats and how they lived a good life on the backs of the hard-working, everyday people. How the Communists had freed us all from that repressed system, and how grateful we should be for our leader, Stalin, who had the wisdom and courage to fight for our equality.

Communism became not just a political doctrine, but a substitute to religion. We were taught that Stalin, our kind and brilliant father, had dedicated his life to teach his children what was right and what was wrong in the world. Every day it was reiterated to us that we needed to religiously follow Stalin's teachings. Anybody who questioned anything in his dogma was severely punished.

We children were important targets of Communist brain-washing. We were told it was our obligation to make sure that our parents were also very loyal and true to our leader. We were to report them immediately if we saw them listening to a foreign radio station, especially Radio Free Europe. We were to tell if we heard them saying anything negative about Stalin or anything against Communism. We were to choose our government over our parents, and our teacher frequently reminded us of it.

I loved my parents too much to report them. I just instinctively knew it was not the thing to do, and my classmates felt the same way, for the most part. However, there was an incident when one of my classmates snitched on her father, simply because she was mad at him. The result of her telling on her father became a tragedy for her family. He disappeared overnight— he was taken out of their home, arrested, and never to be seen again by anyone. Years later, *that poor student* confessed that she had been lying about her father's rebellious acts. She had just wanted to punish him. She had to live with the agony of that lie for the rest of her life.

One day, I learned that my old, blind grandmother was an enemy of the state. Our teacher taught us an easy way to identify the enemies of our people. If their last name ended with a "y," it meant they were from aristocratic blood, and thus, they were greedy landowners who lived off the back of the working class, and they should be punished.

I became very sad, but said nothing, as I remembered my beloved great-grandparents' last name, as well as my grandmother, was Rethy. It ended with a "y."

I went home crying. Mama explained to me that her grandfather was a gentleman farmer with an aristocratic family name that they had inherited from their ancestors of many generations before. Such a name was usually given to them by a king, for some kind of bravery. This knowledge terrified me. How could it be that my beloved great-grandparents, who were so full of kindness and love, were considered enemies of the people?

Mama assured me they were not, and they could not help that they were born to that family. I was deeply concerned about what would happen to them. My mother looked at me with sadness, and finally told me that they were both already gone. Later on in my life, I learned that Russian soldiers were known to go into the homes of aristocrats, kill them, and take over their estates. Being that both of my great-grandparents were dead at the same time, I figured that this might be the case.

My mother told me that they were now safe. They were in Heaven. She also told me that I didn't have to worry about my grandmother, since she had married a commoner and now had a common last name. Then and there, I decided that nobody needed to know our deep family secret.

Later that year, Grandmother died peacefully from complications of pneumonia. I fell into a melancholic state of mind, which lasted for a few months.

MY MOTHER AND HER PARENTS

With Grandmother gone and my parents working long hours, six days a week, I felt very alone. There were no babysitters, and no after-school programs, so my brother and I were alone in the home after school and on weekends. Most of the children in the country were in the same situation.

We were essentially latch-key kids. My little brother spent endless hours playing soccer with his neighborhood friends, so I was very often by myself in the house, usually cold and usually hungry. After I did my homework, I discovered reading, which I really enjoyed. The only problem was that we only had a few books in our home and there were no libraries close. During these lonely times I reminisced back to my great grandparents' house, thinking about their library full of books. I imagined how wonderful it would have been for me to sit in their comfortable library, searching for just the right book to read.

The few books in our home were classic novels, most of them donated to us. Most were translated copies of foreign, Western authors: Balzac, Stendhal, de Maupassant; American writers Pearl Buck and Margaret Mitchell, and a few Hungarian novels about the life and tribulations of the high society.

These books were all declared dissident literature by the Communist state. They were banned by the government – especially the books by American authors.

Friends had given us the books, friends we trusted. We could have been in trouble with the government if these books were ever discovered. Citizens were required to turn in the censored books to the bureaucrats, who in turn burned them. I guess my mother, who was an avid reader if she ever had time, was one of the brave ones who kept them. We had a translated copy of Pearl Buck's *The Good Earth* and Margaret Mitchell's *Gone with the Wind.* I found great delight in the reading of such books; they took me far away to exotic places with stories of interesting people.

***

Grandmother's death had been reported to the Communist bureaucrats. We were now a family of four living in a house with three bedrooms and a kitchen, and it was declared to be much too big for us. Government workers came and assessed our house and the final decision was made: we were required to provide a living space to one more person. We were also forced to give up our kitchen for the government to rent out. My parents had to move our stove to the living/dining room. It was cramped, but doable.

Mama was unhappy with having to take in a stranger. She thought that we should try and trade our suburban garden residence for an apartment in central Budapest. She loved to watch people and be close to the theaters, libraries, and museums. The once-cosmopolitan area appealed to her, even though it wasn't in the glory it had once been in. Papa and I loved the suburbs. We loved the serenity of it, the garden, and the nature all around us.

Mama looked at the advertisements in the paper every day, hoping to find somebody who wanted to exchange their centrally-located apartment for a home in our area. She found a few possible locations, and on Sundays we all went with her to check them out for the possibility of an exchange. Luckily, the options were hideous. Most of them had smaller spaces than we had, and some of them still had walls not repaired from the damage of the war. Some were windowless, dark places, and all of them were shared apartments, which meant more than one family occupied the unit. Mama decided to give up her idea and we stayed in the home. We would just have to learn to accept whomever the government sent to live with us.

There were many horror stories circulating about all kinds of trouble caused by the forced living situations. We heard of fights, people not speaking to each other for years in the same house, stories of having to share a bathroom with strangers chosen by the government.

Now we were facing the same unfortunate fate. Who would they send? Would the person be bearable?

BUDAPEST

SEVEN

Klara the Housemate

They sent a woman named Klara. She was in her late 50's and was considered an old maid because she had never married nor had children. Klara was an artist and her job was to do piece work for the government. She hand-painted animal figures on baby bibs, fruit on aprons, and other intricate creations on clothing that was designated for export. It was an important money source for the state. To my delight, the government allowed her to work at home. Now I had a surrogate mother, a companion, and a teacher. I was thrilled.

Klara allowed me to watch her working and I sensed she might have enjoyed having some company. She was a fascinating woman and had been a well-seasoned traveler before the war. She had amazing stories of adventure, which gave me a glimpse of how life in our country used to be. As an artist, her stories were full of rich detail, and through them, I was able to see through her eyes. I was able to learn about places of which I never even dreamed.

Klara grew up in central Budapest as the daughter of a judge. They owned a townhome there. When the Communists took over and nationalized all private homes, of course their townhome was confiscated. But that was not all. Because her father was a judge, he was considered to be part of the Capitalistic legal system. It also meant he was part of the old regime, and therefore it was decided that he must be punished.

The Communist government wanted everyone to be equal, and they had to come up with a plan to create this equality. As far as they were concerned, it was very unfair that the peasants and farmers lived on farms and had no opportunity to be educated, while all of the highly-educated intellectuals were living in luxury in the cities.

They started human exchanges, to make the people more "equal." All of the intellectuals in Budapest had to leave the city, but without any of their properties, or even their personal items— it all belonged to the state by then. Hundreds of thousands of city people were forced to move out to a very remote farmland to be employed as laborers. The next step was moving the farmers into the city, where their fourth-grade educations were to be improved. They were immediately enrolled into the universities to become architects and engineers (this was better than their Asian or Russian counterparts, who ended up in the labor camps in Siberia or who were murdered by the Communist government.)

Klara and her father were two of the intellectuals selected to leave all of their possessions and be relocated to the depressing, make-shift mass housing in the country. They were assigned to work all day planting, weeding, and gathering produce in remote farmlands. Her father the judge was an elderly retired gentleman, who was both frail and in ill health. Hard work and the hot sun took its toll on his body and in no time he got very ill and died. Klara's mother had died before the war, so now Klara was all alone. Just by luck, one of the bureaucrats discovered her artistic talent and said she was needed by the government. They said she would be relocated to where she was needed, which in that case was close to

Budapest. She of course had no right to her own family's property; she had to move where the government assigned her. That is how Klara ended up living in our kitchen.

Her story was beautiful, sad, and haunting. Before the war, she had followed her passion and her artistic talents, hoping to become a photographer. She went to Italy to enroll in the best school in Europe at the time, to learn the most artistic way of photography. While there, she met and fell in love with a young Italian photographer, to whom she was soon engaged. They started happily planning their wedding when Klara's mother became very ill and she went back to Budapest to be with her. Her mother's illness lingered for a couple of years, and then she died.

After her mother died, she felt her father, who was in deep mourning, needed her. She could not abandon him. She decided to take care of him for a little while. The little while became months, and her fiancé grew tired of waiting for her and broke their engagement. She immediately went back to Italy, but by the time she arrived he was gone. He had enlisted in the army, like most young men did in Europe at that time, with the war on the horizon. She came back to Budapest broken-hearted, just in time to witness the beginning of the war. Her fiancé died in one of the battles.

Listening to Klara's stories opened up a new world that was totally unreachable to me in my life at that time. She was an amazing storyteller. She described the beauty of Italy in precise detail: the canals of Venice, the ancient ruins of Rome, the art in Florence. Her stories were so visual that I could see the narrow, colorful streets and practically smell the risotto cooking.

She taught me Italian operas and many popular songs. She taught me art history, describing in detail the famous artwork hanging in the Louvre in Paris. Sometimes I closed my eyes and literally saw the detail of the art she described. When my husband and I visited Italy forty-five years later, I was amazed at how everything felt so familiar to me.

Klara fulfilled her obligations and painted those clothes for hours, and as I watched her and listened to her, I learned something very important. I learned from her that there was more to the world than the narrow life the Communists had created for us.

Klara and I never once discussed anything about Communism. She didn't need to criticize it for me to see the difference between a good life and tyranny. Just hearing her stories spoke volumes to me. From Klara's stories, I learned the difference and, even as a young child, could see the contrast. I was suddenly aware that I was not free to see the world as I was meant to see it. I was not free to be what I wanted to be. My generation's future was bleak. I was destined to work in a dark grey factory on a forced, assigned job, day in and day out, just like my father did, working so hard but not earning enough money to feed and clothe his family. I would never be able to see the wonders of the world as a prisoner of a crazy demagogue's society, where we were pushed to be equal puppets in a truly slave-like existence.

Stalin had famously said, "Give me a five-year-old and I will make him a true communist for life." Well, I had been that five-year-old, and I had been submerged deeply in his rhetoric, but it did not stick. It only took one woman's story of her experience in the free world for me to see the truth and realize the lies, the atrocity, and the inhuman dogma of what Communism really was. In the coming years, as I grew into a young teenager, I never talked to anybody about my newfound feelings except my mother and father.

Klara moved away a few years later. She had a distant cousin whose husband passed away, and she got permission from the government to go live with her. Finally she could be with family. I lost contact with her through the years, but I always hoped she knew how much she had influenced my life, how much I admired her. How much I appreciated her opening my eyes to see the real truth. And most of all, I appreciated her teaching me that the idea of being free to see the world's wonders was the noblest idea of all.

EIGHT

The Secret Police

Western Europe, with its free enterprise system and private property ownership laws, was built back quickly after the war. They also received great financial help from the United States with the Marshall Plan. But Hungary became one of the satellites of the Communist Soviet Union, and as such it was forced to reject American aid, by order of the Soviet government.

Hungary's bridges were built back after the war, and the public transportation was put back in full operation, but most of the buildings, especially if they were habitable, were not repaired. The city still showed a lot of damage.

It looked terrible and somber, a shadow of its former beauty.

The people of Budapest were overworked, undernourished, and very poorly dressed. They were under a burden of poverty, hardship, worry, and despair. The country fell into second world status. The evidence of a failed economic experiment of forced commerce was everywhere.

Not only did any of the private citizens own homes, apartments, or buildings, but they had no interest, money, or authority to repair or repaint the places they now lived. Everything belonged to the government, and the bureaucrats controlled every aspect of life very tightly.

The real hardship was more than poverty; it was the loss of freedom. We were living with no freedom to have contact with the outside world, no freedom to travel. We had no free speech, no property rights, and no right to have a fair trial in a fair justice system. There was no freedom to innovate and no freedom to own a business.

In the free market system of capitalist countries, millions of individuals decide for themselves what to farm or produce. They decided what to distribute and how much to sell it for. This of course created millions of goods that their society needed and wanted, and their society, in turn, made purchases based on their individual needs. Our Communist government controlled all aspects of commerce, and they never had enough information on the market prices of goods, so they couldn't effectively ration out our country's resources. There was no way they could know the needs of each individual, so they just came up with something that they thought was suitable. It didn't matter that we all had different wants, different needs, different temperaments, and different levels of ambition and drive. Their way of "equalizing" human nature was with force, and with force we lost our freedom to be individual and unique.

Communism was supposedly designed to bring us freedom from the upper-crust, intellectual, profit-seeking industrialists. Ironically, it was dreamed up by a privileged, intellectual man named Karl Marx and his industrial partner, Friedrich Engels. Communists had their top bureaucrats take over the most luxurious homes in the city. They not only had cars, but there were rumors that they had secret stores packed with merchandise that was not available for the general population.

Those egotistical men, and their comrades in

top management, had unbelievable power and ultimate control over all of us. They had secret police and gatekeepers called ÁVO (which translates to the "Hungarian State Police State Protection Department"), who they paid better than the average citizen, and who probably earned bonuses finding the "enemies." Their target could be anybody who was not satisfied with the system. Their job was to terrorize and control the masses, making sure no one went against them. They were on par with the Russian KGB. The ÁVO were really a secret. You didn't always know who they were. Your next door neighbor could be an ÁVO agent; a stranger walking past your window could be an ÁVO agent.

At any time or any place, you could be asked for identification. Citizens were instructed to carry their identification card with them at all times, even when they were just walking somewhere. No one had a car, so everybody walked. If you were in a hurry, you looked suspicious. If you were in another part of the city far away from your residence, you had better have a good explanation for it. Of course the real reason the police were present was so people wouldn't gather together and discuss their dissatisfaction or come up with a way to overthrow them.

These "policemen" were usually appointed by the local Communist leaders. They got paid if they brought in someone they felt was an enemy of the system. The accused citizen's wrongdoing did not have to be proven. As a result, many innocent people lost their freedom or their lives.

We quickly learned not to trust anybody, not even our own friends. Desperation, poverty, and the chance to earn more money brought out the worst in some people. The city was full of policemen, which in most places is a blessing that represents peace and order, but in the Communist regime it meant harassment.

We weren't allowed to learn any Western languages. My parents spoke three languages, and I spoke German and Hungarian when I was a child. Learning Russian was mandatory, and forced on every student, but none of our teachers spoke any Russian, so they couldn't effectively teach it. They distributed very poorly -designed and poorly-written text books, instructing us to memorize endless lists of words and meaningless grammar.

One day, when I was in about seventh grade, our teacher informed us that we had to go to an assembly for a very important event. We walked to the neighboring park, where all of the area's school students were gathered. There must have been several hundred students present. First we were instructed, as always, to honor our teacher, Comrade Stalin. Then all of a sudden a boy from my neighborhood named Andy was asked to go to the podium.

The school principal informed us that Andy was a misguided student who had committed an inexcusable act, and needed to be severely punished. He was going to be used as an example for the rest of us.

Then the big announcement was made. Because of the serious crime he had committed, he was being thrown out of school. He was not just expelled from our school, but he was blackballed from every school in the city. And not just the city, the *country*.

What was his unforgivable crime? He drew a beard and glasses over a picture of Comrade

Joseph Stalin in one of his textbooks.

The punishment did not end there. His father had to serve two years in jail. What was his father's crime? He did not teach his son to properly respect our dear leader, Stalin.

My elementary school years went by year after year, uneventfully. Our lives remained monotonous and dull.

Stalin died in the spring of 1953. He was discovered snoring on the floor in his pajamas, in a coma. He had been drinking his usual red wine the night before, and many people thought the wine had been poisoned. He had suffered a stroke, which eventually caused him to suffocate. After his death, there was a scramble between his top people to figure out which of them was to replace him.

His death meant some changes in Hungary.

Some of the forced labor ended; some of the prisoners were released. Our country developed a reform wing, and a man named Imre Nagy replaced Rákosi. We hoped things would get better, but we soon found out that Rákosi was still in the government as the General Secretary, and he very often sabotaged Nagy's reform plans. Things ended up staying pretty much the same— but there was one thing that was changing.

My father.

NINE

The Opportunity

As my elementary school years came to a close, I noticed my father was changing. Year after year, he became more and more vocal against the Communist government.

Once in a while there were a few brave men who attempted to challenge the system, and it always meant that they had to face very serious consequences. The challenger was immediately labeled as the enemy of the people and he had to be "eliminated" - which meant be killed or put in jail. But even these possibilities didn't stop my father from showing his distaste for Communism.

There was a mandatory town meeting one

night, and our local leader asked Mama to volunteer to do something for them the following Sunday. Papa stood up and said, "I don't think my wife will have time next Sunday, because in this great system I only have money to buy one pair of underwear and she has to wash them on Sundays."

My mother and I were terrified. We were waiting for the ÁVO to come to pick him up and put him in jail, but nobody came. It was probably brushed away as a stupid statement. But it was not far off the mark. I had only one piece of clothing next to the one uniform I had to wear every day. Mama hand washed it every Saturday night after work, and we prayed it would dry on the line by Monday morning, before I had to wear it for school again. Clothes were always completely unaffordable. As we children grew out of our clothes, Mama took them apart and re-sewed them, adding additional material to them. She did that as many times as possible, until they completely fell apart, and then she made braided rugs out of them. I remember my mother wearing one grey flannel skirt during all of those years. My father couldn't help but point out the fact that we owned very little clothing.

I wondered if his new boldness was due to the fact that he was listening to more and more broadcasts of *Radio Free Europe,* which was also called *Radio Liberty.* He listened to the banned station every night. It was a bold move, as *Radio Free Europe* was strictly banned.

The radio station, funded in part by the United States, was broadcast from Munich, Germany, during that time. It provided music and literature that were banned in our country, but more importantly, it provided uncensored news to its listeners, including details on anti-communist protests. The station brought my father hope by demonstrating that a more robust and trustworthy world existed beyond the Iron Curtain. It showed him that other countries believed Communism to be a totally immoral system of government.

When he was still alive, Stalin had personally ordered our government to try to block those radio broadcasts by "jamming"- deliberately transmitting radio signals that disrupted the station by decreasing the signal-to-noise ratio. It still came through on our radio, and my father continued to listen to it. I was so worried that someone would hear it, and my father would be jailed, or worse. Luckily, the house in which we resided had huge limestone walls, making it virtually sound-proof. Our neighbors were also a good distance away. Still, I was worried we would be caught. I constantly looked out of the windows to make sure nobody was near.

As the time approached for me to finish my eighth year of elementary school, my upcoming future started to concern me. Poor nutrition had caused my immune system to be very weak, and I had missed a lot of school as a result. I'd had scarlet fever, pneumonia, and strep throat infections. I had once contracted a virus that almost developed into tuberculosis, and I had to stay in bed for two months, needing monthly chest x-rays for years after that.

Our government provided eight years of free general education to all students, and after that, most of them went to a technical or occupational school. They then became things like cooks, mechanics, or barbers. As I listened to my classmates' choices, I realized I had a higher ambition and higher expectations for myself. I didn't want to stop there at eighth grade. I wanted to keep going — I wanted more education.

I very much wanted to go to high school to further my education, but I wasn't sure how to go about doing so. The school never provided us with any counsel to inform us for our possibilities and choices. And even if they had, I certainly wasn't at the top of my class with all of the days of school I had missed due to being sick.

One day I decided to chance it. I had nothing to lose. I went and asked the principal if it would be possible for me to go to the high school. I considered her a fair woman, so I sat and awaited her answer.

She looked at me, and then looked at my

grades.

She looked at me again. There was a silence.

Then she spoke.

"You do not have the best grades..."

I held my breath.

"But I can see on your face that you are very determined. Let me see what I can do."

She left the room.

I sat there wondering what she would come back and say.

When she returned to the room she said, "There is only one choice for you— and we need to get you in quickly because there are only two spots open."

She smiled, saying, "It is a good choice. Either

you can be trained as a statistician and work for the Statistical Institute or you can become a bookkeeper. The school is not far from here. I can call them now if you are interested."

I got very excited, and told her that the subject of statistics did interest me a great deal, because it was people-oriented. A statistician's job would be to find out things such as how long the population lived, how many babies were born in a certain time period, how many people were married and so on. I thought it would be fascinating.

"I will arrange it for you right away."

From our class of twenty-four, I was one of two students who moved on to ninth grade. I was surprised. I had constantly heard the Communists boasting of how they were providing free "higher education" to all. Higher education may have been free, but it was certainly not pushed, and definitely not available to all.

I was lucky to have made it there.

I was terrifically excited that fall. It took forty minutes by tram for me to get to the school, but I didn't mind— I figured I would use it to study. There were three ninth grade freshman classes; I was assigned to class C. There were twenty-six students in my class. Surprisingly, only three of us lived in the city, and the rest of the students were from far-away small towns. They all lived in the dormitories. I was curious why they chose a school so far from their homes and families. They told me they *didn't* choose to, it was chosen *for* them. They were told it was "in their best interest" to attend, which was always a veiled threat. The social engineering of equalization was still being practiced, and that came with discrimination toward me, the girl from the city. It dawned on me that all of the city kids I knew had ended school at eighth grade or were being sent to trade schools; and the country kids from farms were continuing on to get higher education. Technically, I didn't belong there. But I had slipped in, and I was eternally grateful for that spot in the class.

High school was very demanding. We had to attend school six days a week, a half hour for lunch, and one ten-minute break. Classes started at 8 a.m. and went to 3 p.m. The students stayed in the same classroom, but the teachers changed every hour. All classes were mandatory— there were seven academic classes, along with Russian language, Political Science, and P.E. There were only three business classes, three times a week. There was a lot of homework as well— it was not for the weak.

The rules were very stringent. We were to enroll in the Youth Communist Party, no questions asked. If we did not enroll, they would not let us finish high school. It was absolutely required. We had to wear a navy blue uniform every day, and even our text books had to be covered uniformly in an indigo-colored paper. There was a long list of forbidden activities we had to obey: No serious dating, no going anywhere where alcohol was served, or even to the coffee houses. I was not a social butterfly by nature, so these rules didn't bother me much.

There was precisely one day in my entire school career where the Political Science teacher talked about capitalism. I always thought of this particular teacher as a pure Communist, so this was surprising to me.

He did not speak on the evil of capitalism that day— it was quite the contrary. He told us about how the free enterprise system worked in the United States. He told us that in that system, someone could invent, say, a better can opener. Then that person could get a patent on it and sell that can opener. If people liked his product, they would buy it. He could make millions.

I was completely fascinated by what he said. *Wow!* You were free to *invent* something, anything you wanted? And you could then make your *own money* off of it? And the government *let* you do it? It was *legal?* That was the very first time in my life I had ever heard the concept of the free enterprise system. I had no idea what his intention was in telling us about it, and I was sure he could get in trouble for telling us. But he certainly made a huge impression on me and it was a very memorable moment. I remember thinking, *That system is for me.*

We had been listening to years of Communist propaganda by that time, about how horrible the capitalist system was, how the factory owners took advantage of the workers, how the workers had to fight for their money, how people struggled to live in such an unfair, unequal society. It was right then and there in that classroom when it truly hit me.

All of that propaganda was a pure lie.

At that moment, our teacher backtracked a little and threw in some business about how the capitalistic factory owners often abused the poor workers, but I had heard enough. The thought that someone could achieve something like that, the thought that someone could come up with their own idea and bring it to the marketplace for the consumer. For some reason I got very excited about that idea. The idea that someone could enjoy the fruit of their labor. The idea that whatever you invented did not belong to the state.

And then my heart sank. I knew that in our country, there were no incentives for anyone to invent anything. It was an impossible dream for any of us to live in such a way, with such freedom. We would all live and die in the "Workers' Paradise," where everybody was equal.

Equally poor.

We all were prisoners in our country. Prisoners of the tyrants, in the name of "just" equality. Nobody needed to *excel* in Communism. Nobody needed to invent. I thought about it for weeks.

One evening, I got up the courage to ask my father about it.

"How was our economic system before the war? Before Communism?" I asked.

He looked at me with alarm. He was caught off guard. He wasn't expecting me to ask such a thing.

"Why do you ask?"

I told him what I learned in my class and what I thought about it. He said it was all true—except that it wasn't quite as easy as it sounded to invent something and make millions, but that yes, that was basically the way it worked.

I knew he had once embraced the Communist ideology, before the war. He had welcomed the Communist system, like all of the other millions who were waiting for a good, equal, and just life.

"Papa...You have been complaining about Communism for *years* now. If it was so much better before Communism...why did you become a Communist?"

He looked at me with sad eyes.

"We were idealistic. I read Marx's work and it sounded great— collective manufacturing, distributing the profits to the workers rather than having just one man enjoy it all— that idea appealed to us. We truly had no idea what we had gotten ourselves into. We traded our good lives. We used to be paid enough money to live a comfortable life. We were not rich, but we were free, and it was pleasant. This centrally planned system, where nobody knows what they are doing, and the leaders are arrogant

Communist dictators, is far worse. The very sad part is that under this system, it was not only that we lost a way of earning a good living, but we lost the freedom to express our feelings. We have become slaves. Terrorized slaves."

MAGYAR
POSTA
1 Ft

TEN

Comrade Isti

I was at one of the mandatory Young Communist Party meetings one day, when my life suddenly became more complicated.

The particular Communist leader in charge of our school was a downright vicious person. He loved his power and loved to terrorize whomever he could. His first name was Istvan, but everyone called him Comrade Isti. I think he preferred that nick name, because the word was so close to "Isten," which means God in Hungarian. He was tall and intimidating, with a muscular build and a huge, reddish mustache. His large, dark eyes were both piercing and threatening.

I was leaving after a meeting that particular day and he called me back to him. I was scared out of my wits. What had I done? Why would he single me out? This couldn't be good.

"I want you to stay. I need to have a word with you," he said.

Slowly the large room emptied as I watched all of the people leaving. He carefully finished gathering all of his papers. He then lit a cigarette. It must of have been ten or fifteen minutes that went by, but it felt like an eternity to me. He slowly stood up and motioned to me to approach his desk, to let me know he was ready for me.

He saw the terror in my eyes, and I could see he truly enjoyed every minute of his power over me. Very slowly and bluntly he said, "You know you are not eligible to be educated in the People's School of Hungary."

My stomach dropped.

My education! No! I need this education! I thought.

He took a long puff of his cigarette and watched the whirling smoke he blew out disappear into the thin air.

Here it is. We are done. My family is over. We are exposed. It has finally happened.

"I found out both of your grandmothers were from aristocratic families. That makes you a descendent of the aristocrats. What do you have to say about this?"

I said, "I can't help what family I was born into." I said it as gently as possible in order not to make him angry. "And besides, my father is a

Communist."

"He WAS a Communist," he corrected me, "and we are watching him very closely."

I must have become very pale. I felt close to fainting from the stress of the situation.

Slowly he continued in a very threatening voice, "At this time, I won't tell the authorities about it, since you only have one year left of high school. But you have to prove to me that you have redeemed yourself. You will have to pay for the sins of your ancestors for taking advantage of us, the proletariats."

Part of the Communist regime was of course getting rid of the professionals, the intellectuals: the "bourgeois" class. Thousands of these people, who were not unlike my great-grandparents, were forced out of their homes and off of their property, "purged" from the country. I knew that in this man's Communist mind, I was the enemy of the people. I had heard that kind of speech from him in many meetings before and in school since I was seven years old.

I again got lightheaded and tried to stop myself from fainting. My breathing was shallow.

"May I sit down?" I asked.

He motioned me to the closest chair.

In that moment I thought my world, my hope and my freedom had ended. I knew well the strength of his power. Would we be imprisoned? Executed?

I had heard plenty about what happened to those former professionals, or aristocrats— now considered "enemies." The possibility of being punished was real; it was the destiny of some of the people living around me. I had heard that my beloved great-grandparents were killed by Russian soldiers right after the war in Romania. It was common for soldiers to go into large homes and kill the occupants.

Was it now my turn, our turn? Would we be next to be punished? I knew full well that the punishment wouldn't be decided by a judge or a jury— it would be decided by Comrade Isti himself. He had the power to make or break my life at that moment, the lives of my family. We had been lucky so many times before, I didn't think we could get lucky yet again, this had to be it. We had to have run out of luck. This had to be the time where we ended up like so many other Hungarians, in prison camps, or dead.

"I understand. What can I do?" I said meekly.

"You have asked a good question," he said in a

more calm voice. "There is a lot of paperwork that has to be done here. Come over tomorrow after school and my secretary will give you the workload. Make sure you finish it promptly. I also want you to study more on the struggle and suffering of the people by the bourgeoisies through the centuries. Study the works of our teacher, Comrade Stalin, and Lenin, who saved us from the varmints."

He went to his desk and pulled out a printed piece of paper.

"Here is the list. You must buy these books and read them."

I looked at the list. It had maybe five books on it.

"I will. Thank you."

"I see you are cooperating; there is hope for you,

comrade," he said with an awkward smile.

"Yes," I said.

"You can go now."

I left quickly, before he changed his mind. I walked out onto what was by then a dark street. I passed a church, and my first thought was that I should go in and pray, go and give thanks to God for the outcome of the night. Quickly I looked around; there were a few people walking by. There was no way I could go into a church. I couldn't take any more chances. If I did anything that the Communists didn't like, I would pay for it dearly. I would lose my chance to be educated. I would lose my future, my freedom, or my life.

In the next few weeks, I did the administrative work Isti asked of me. Luckily, he was not in the office most of the time. I tried very hard to avoid him in any way I could. I was relieved that he never asked about the books he made me buy and read, and happy I didn't run into him often, but I was in *constant* fear. It hung over me, always in the background of my life, always heavy on my heart: this man could say the word, and my whole family could be in severe danger. The thought that he could change his mind and turn us in at any moment, filled me with horror. The whole system was so preposterous, that I knew it didn't matter what was true and what wasn't. If this man said we were the enemies, we were over. I felt this petrifying responsibility, hoping that I wouldn't anger him, hoping that I did a good job of the things he asked. I wouldn't be able to forgive myself if I made a wrong move and destroyed the lives of my family. It was a mental burden that became part of my existence.

While I was living with that dread, the world was changing around me. Austria had come up with a treaty that established them as independent, democratic, and free. They banned Fascism. Soviet troops left Austria, making it a spot close to us that offered freedom. We never thought something like that could happen so close to us.

The thought on the minds of many Hungarians was the same: *Could our country do the same thing?*

THE CARPATHIANS

ELEVEN

The Officer's Coat

It was the end of June, 1956, and I had just finished my junior year of high school. It was a grueling last few weeks because we had both written and oral final exams. The oral exams were especially stressful, especially the one I had coming up on the last day of the week: Chemistry. I felt unusually tired and ill on the day of the exam and it didn't help that a) Chemistry wasn't one of my strong suits, and b) while I had worked very hard to study my chemistry book, I hadn't gotten to the last chapter.

Our oral tests were given by a panel of teachers, including our very strict chemistry teacher, who had us pull a random piece of folded paper from a basket and speak on the book chapter it listed.

Please don't let me pull the last chapter...please... It's the only one I don't know...

I promised God if He let me pull any other chapter other than the last chapter I would take my time to learn it even if the test was over and I never needed to know anything in that chapter for the rest of my life.

Luckily I chose a chapter I knew well. I did a masterful presentation, ignoring my sore throat and harsh cough. By the time I boarded the tram I could tell I had a fever. I got home and went to bed immediately, bringing my chemistry book to study the promised chapter. My eyes started to water and I had a hard time breathing. When my mother came home she found me asleep with a very high fever.

I was worse the next morning. Mama gave me some cough medicine and some aspirin and I started to feel a little better. She left to go to work and I stayed in bed alone all day, I had no energy to move. My coughing became worse and my breathing was very heavy and difficult. By the time Mama came back home I told her I knew death was near for me. I had never ever felt so sick. I was gasping for air with barely any energy left in my body.

My father and brother arrived shortly thereafter, and Mama was frantic. She wanted one of them to run and get a doctor, but we had no telephone to call one. Papa went and got someone, but by the time he arrived, my fever was up to 105 degrees. He diagnosed me as having pneumonia, and he promptly gave me a penicillin injection and told us if the penicillin didn't work within an hour that I needed to be taken to the hospital. The doctor stayed with me for about two hours, and luckily the penicillin worked, my breathing got easier and my fever broke. I had just survived an acute pneumonia infection, my third one, and it took me a few weeks to recover.

That spring, the First Secretary of the Communist Party of the Soviet Union, Nikita Khrushchev, had surprised everybody. He gave what was known as the "secret speech" to Communist Party Delegates in a closed-session meeting. He more or less blasted Stalin and his unfair and evil ways, criticizing the way he had run the government.

By late spring we saw some small differences in our government. Citizens were now allowed to apply for visas to visit their close relatives, as long as their relatives lived in another Communist country. My father was very excited. His mother and sister had stayed back in old Hungary, which was now part of Romania. He hadn't seen them for fourteen years. Traveling had been forbidden, he was not even allowed to travel to attend his father's funeral five years prior.

Papa immediately applied for a visa. We didn't have enough money for all four of us to go, but we had enough in our emergency account for three of us. My mother said she would stay behind and let us go. She did not mind, she understood.

The government had also come up with a new rule that was meant to help us: we were allowed to bring back a small amount of products from other countries— but it had to be for personal use or sold to friends only. It was refreshing good news. We hoped that we might find something that would provide us with an additional way to supplement the cost of our train fare.

The last time I had seen my paternal grandmother I was two years old, much too young to remember her.

MY MOTHER AND I AS A BABY VISITING MY FRATERNAL GRANDPARENTS AND AUNT BEFORE THE WAR

My brother had never met her. It was an exciting time. We were going on a vacation and we would have a reunion with relatives. We were only a little sad that Mama couldn't be there to enjoy it with us.

The trip was glorious. My grandmother and aunt also lived in the countryside of the Carpathian Mountains, just as my mother's great-grandparents had. We saw the deep green forest, the rushing rivers, and the shimmering, pristine lake. Beautiful meadows were bursting with wild flowers celebrating the summer.

Romania was a communist satellite of Russia that year, so economically it was in much better shape than Hungary. Romania's wealth had considerably increased when they received a large portion of Hungarian territory with fertile land and natural riches of oil, gold, and silver.

The house my grandmother and aunt shared was small but pleasant and impeccably orderly and clean. It had a wonderful, bright summer room, with wall-to-wall French windows overlooking the dahlia garden. A well-scrubbed old pine farm table was set in the middle of the room. We had our meals there.

My widowed grandmother was an amazing woman; she was like several Martha Stewarts rolled into one. Her garden was the finest I had ever seen, she grew everything. She even made her own raspberry wine, as well as various other liquors and vinegars. Her pastries rivaled any fine Parisian pastry chef's ritzy creations. She was capable of anything and everything, doing it all with beauty and class.

She became an orphan at an early age, but nobody ever talked about what had happened, as people in those days always avoided speaking of anything unpleasant. I had one small clue as to her parents when she showed me her family crest that she had kept. Her father had been an aristocrat, and that is about all I learned of him. Her only brother was a physician, but he lived in a distant city, and I never met him.

My kind aunt was a slender, small woman with cascading, chestnut-color hair. She had become a widow at a very young age. Her handsome military officer husband was taken to fight the war in Russia right after they were married and had died in a fearsome battle in the city of Odessa in 1944. After her husband's death, she decided she needed to find a way to become financially independent. She enrolled in college courses and worked her way to a diploma. She was an accountant when we met her; she did the entire payroll for the local gold mine.

She was flawlessly dressed in a freshly-ironed

pastel linen dress one morning and I complimented her on it. She said most of her dresses she had acquired before the war. She took me to her large armoire and opened it. There were rows of flowered silk dresses and stunning solid linens, all arranged by color. At the end of the row was an olive green, wool coat.

"Is that is your winter coat?" I asked.

"No, my winter clothes are in the other armoire. That was my husband's officer coat. I keep it for a memory of him," she smiled softly.

I took the coat out, and felt its luxurious wool fabric. It was so thick and soft that I wished I could own a coat like that.

"Try it on," she said, reading my mind.

I put my arms through the sleeves and it hung

on me. It was much too big and long, but so extravagantly soft. I had never had anything so luxurious on my body in my life.

"It's too big on me," I said, secretly disappointed.

"Yes of course," she said, "but it can be made to fit. It can be hemmed, made double breasted, and the shoulders could be taken in a little...it could be wearable. Something too big has more potential than something too small..."

She eyed it on me and smiled.

"Are you giving this to me?" I asked.

"I can't think of a better use of my dear husband's coat than to know my lovely niece is using it. It is new, he never wore it. He ordered it just before he was deployed, and of course he never came back to wear it."

I was so proud of that army coat and the fact that it had belonged to my brave uncle from Romania. It had sat there for over twelve years, and now it was mine, soft and lavish. I was thrilled at my aunt's generosity.

My father, brother and I looked around Romania for a product that Hungary did not have; something we could take back with us. We found black pepper all over Romania, and our country had none. We decided it would be our investment, so we purchased about five pounds of it. The store clerk told us she had heard through the grapevine that people were not having any trouble getting it back over the border. We were happy to hear that.

When it was time to leave, we said our goodbyes, hugged, kissed and waved. I had no idea that it was the last time I would ever see my grandmother and aunt again.

We were a little melancholy when we left our ancestral land and our relatives, and also a little nervous to be carrying the five pounds of black pepper. But the store clerk had been right, the border patrol man just nodded when they saw the pepper as they went through our luggage. He said that antiques or historical objects were the things they were looking for; those things couldn't be brought out of the country. It was the same on the Hungarian side.

We took the rare black pepper back to our neighborhood and found that we had made an excellent choice. We sold it all within a week because it was such a hot commodity. Our first and only entrepreneurial endeavor had been a success. Our friends were delighted to have some black pepper on their food, and we made enough money to cover part of our trip. It was a win/win situation. We got back to Budapest just two weeks before my senior year started.

I showed my mother my new olive green coat. She worked very hard to make it fit me, changing the buttons, fixing the sleeves and shortening the hem. It was still big on me, but it made me very happy because it was the most soft and warm coat I had ever had. There was no fabric that fine available in Budapest; no coat so well-made. I considered myself fortunate to have it and knew it would keep me warm in the coming winter months.

I'd had a wonderful summer. I was so happy to have gotten to know my extended family, and so happy I had survived having pneumonia.

I decided that I would be extra disciplined with my studies in my senior year and try to graduate with all honors. In mid-September, any of us who were interested in pursuing opportunities at the Statistical Institute were invited to visit. It was an exciting day for me. Finally there were good things to look forward to; I would soon have the chance to earn my own living, the chance to contribute to my parents after all of the years that they had taken care of me.

The Institute was on the very top floors of the highest, most prestigious building in Buda. Walking through the offices was thrilling. Our guide, who seemed to be very happy to work there, mentioned that taking college courses on the side would help our chances in securing a job there. The woman took us to a room and showed us the first and only electronic digital storing system in Hungary known as a computer. It was an American Univac, three stories high, and it counted the statistical information with limit cards, traveling fast on speedy rotating rollers from one station to the next. I was so very impressed and wanted nothing more than to work in such a technologically advanced place.

I went home, excited, relieved, and very optimistic of my future.

TWELVE

The Revolution

It was October 22, 1956, and I was traveling home from school on the tram. Having traveled on it for a few years by that time, I had made friends with the other regular travelers. There were two young men who were college students attending a university close to my high school, who I thought were funny and smart. I loved to listen to their witty conversations; it was a fun way to spend travel time when I wasn't studying.

I noticed that in the previous weeks, their usual light-hearted conversations had turned somewhat serious and secretive. Apparently, a few class lectures at the university had turned into a political discussion, and some of the students had gone as far as to criticize the Communist system, mainly the lack of freedom of speech. Many of the local college students, unbeknownst to me, had started attending further intellectual forums to discuss our country's issues. They called the forums Petőfi circles, and they started to attract thousands of people. Mátyás Rákosi had resigned earlier that year, and that appeared to have started a conversation among not just college students, but many journalists and writers to be more involved in politics and more involved in their rights.

On that particular day on the tram, my two college friends were in a fiery conversation about politics with some other young men I had never seen before. They were from the Budapest

University of Technology and Economics. One of them spotted me and immediately put a printed sheet in my hand. It said *Sixteen Points of Demands by the Students.*

“What is this all about?” I asked.

Ignoring my question, he said, “We would like you to join us tomorrow in the late afternoon. University students have organized to meet in Buda at the square end of the Chain Bridge, by the Józef Bem Statue. Please join us; we would like to have a sizable crowd. The flyer you are holding lists the student’s demands. Péter Veres, the President of the Writers’ Union, will read our Sixteen Points. After the speech we are planning to collectively walk across the Chain Bridge to the Parliament to demonstrate.”

A few weeks prior, college students from Szeged, one of our country’s largest cities, had made a bold move. They had completely disregarded the official Communist Student Union and re-established their former democratic student union (Union of Hungarian University and Academy Students) which had been banned by Rákosi. Other student bodies soon did the same. This caused more stirring, more whispering, more talking about reform. The idea of demanding the opportunity of free speech started to travel through Budapest Universities like a wildfire.

The enthusiasm and passion of those students on the tram was exhilarating. It was something pure, something true, and something real to all of us. I knew I wanted to be part of that fight. It was the basic right of any human. We had been living without it for so long that we had accepted it. I was a little scared, but ultimately excited that we were now coming together. It was a rush of emotion and adrenaline. Could we really make a difference? Could we make something happen?

With each various stop that day, more people left the tram, until it was just my two college friends and me.

“I didn’t realize you guys felt the same way about this system as I did. Why haven’t you told me? Why have we never discussed this?”

“Discuss it? With *you*?” asked the boy nicknamed Plain Tall, because he was six feet three inches tall.

“What is wrong with *me*?” I asked.

“We have seen what a good Communist you are at the Youth Communist Party meetings.”

I started to laugh.

"I had to be! My education depended it on it! Comrade Isti was watching me, I had no other choice."

The tram stopped again, and it was my turn to get out.

"I will be there tomorrow, I promise!" I yelled from the street.

"Good, we are counting on you!" they said.

That evening I tried to double up on my homework, so I could be free the next afternoon, but the amount was much too large for me to handle in one evening. I became exhausted and could not keep my eyes open. Mama and Papa were not home, but I promised myself I would tell them about the demonstration in the morning.

I woke up a little late and groggy on Tuesday,

October 23. I washed and dressed as fast as I could. It was a cold morning, so I put on my cap and my olive green army coat and grabbed a couple of lard sandwiches that I had made the night before. I only had five minutes to catch my scheduled tram and had just a few seconds left to say goodbye to Mama as I ran out of the house with my books. Papa had already left for work.

I ate one of the sandwiches on the tram, and took out the crumpled flyer from my jacket pocket. A middle-aged man got on and sat next to me. I immediately folded the paper back up and hid it in the bottom of my bag. It was my big secret. Being afraid was deeply embedded in my psyche.

My classes at school went as scheduled. I didn't have much time to think about the demonstration, and of course I said nothing to anyone. I felt privileged to have been invited by the college students and their friends. I wondered how many of us were going to be there. Maybe a hundred, I guessed.

When school ended, I rushed to the main plaza to catch the tram to the demonstration. I was immediately surprised at how unusually filled it was. Normally it didn't get busy until the rush hour of 5 or 6 p.m.

The tram traveled adjacent to the river and at every stop more and more people wanted to get on, but it was too jam-packed. Finally, it arrived at my stop, but it was so crowded that I was afraid I would not be able to get out in time before the doors closed and it went on to the next stop. I asked the people next to me to let me out, but they all said they were getting out also.

It took me a minute to realize, but an amazing thing had happened. The entire tram emptied out. *Do we all have the same idea? Are we all really going to the same place? Do these people think like I do?*

Could it ***be****?*

As I approached the plaza, it felt like hundreds of people joined me. It was an amazing sight to witness the sea of people gathering. Thousands of students had gathered together in one hour and the crowed quickly swelled to close to twenty thousand people after the workers joined in. It was a pure miracle. No propaganda, no advertising, other than word of mouth and the flyers secretly passed. It started out with a few courageous organizers and soon everyone was joining in. I looked for my college friends in the crowd, but never saw them because there were so many people.

The president of the Writer's Union, Péter Veres, did actually read those Sixteen Points. In a nutshell, the demands were:

1. We demand immediate evacuation of all Soviet troops.

2. We demand a new election by secret ballot for a new Central Committee.

3. We demand a new government under the direction of Imre Nagy, and dismissal of all Communists. No one who has worked for Rákosi or Stalin is to stay.

4. We demand an investigation into the criminal activities of Rákosi and the other government officials who ruined Hungary.

5. We demand a new National Assembly election, with all political parties participating. Workers need the right to strike.

6. We demand revision and re-adjustment in political and cultural affairs.

7. We demand complete reorganization of Hungary's economic life.

8. We demand all foreign trade agreements and the exact total of unpaid reparations be made public. Hungary needs to have the right to sell uranium freely at world market prices to obtain hard currency.

9. We demand radical adjustment of salaries and a minimum living wage for workers.

10. We demand reorganization of the system of distribution. Agricultural products need to be utilized in a rational manner. There needs to be quality of treatment for individual farms.

11. We demand reviews by independent tribunals of all political and economic trials, as

well as the release of all prisoners of war and any innocent parties who were unjustly imprisoned.

12. We demand recognition of freedom of opinion and of expression; of freedom of the press and of radio, as well as the creation of a daily newspaper for the college students.

13. We demand immediate removal of the statue of Stalin.

14. We demand new uniforms for the Army with our Hungarian emblems restored.

15. The students of the Technological University of Budapest declare their solidarity with the workers and students of Warsaw in their movement towards national independence.

16. College Students will be organizing a Youth Parliament in which Hungary's youth will be represented by their delegates.

The crowd had erupted in cheers. Veres continued to speak about how Hungary should have freedom. How it should be democratic. How we no longer needed to be slaves. We needed our land back. We needed to be able to have our own businesses. The crowd kept chanting and cheering, praising those words.

Wonderful patriotic poems were recited. There were tears in all of our eyes when the crowd started to sing our old national hymn. Somebody cut out the Communist symbol from the middle of our national flag, and left a big hole in the middle, which become the symbol of the revolution. Many people did the same to other flags, until there was a sea of flags with holes waving on that cool October

THE DEMONSTRATION, OCTOBER 23, 1956

day. They represented all of the people who were pacified, who'd had their rights stolen, their lives stripped of individuality, their mouths closed, their land stolen, their churches closed, their schools taken over, their dignity taken, and their lives crushed.

It was time to cross the bridge to the Parliament, which was adjacent to the Danube on the Pest side of the city. I saw crowds of people heading that way and realized if I entered the sea of people I would not get home until very, very late. I wasn't sure how late it would all run, or what would become of any of it, and I had to keep my grades up. I had to study and do homework. I left to get back on the tram, my heart full of hope.

I did not know it at the time, but the students had tried to enter the city's main broadcasting station to read their demands on the air. The police held them there, but when people started to crowd outside to call for their release hours later, the police started shooting at the crowd.

One of the government officials tried to shut down the demonstration, which only caused all of the protestors to tear down the large statue of Stalin that they had mentioned in their Sixteen Points. More and more crowds were growing around Hungary, and it got to the point where more people were being shot and tear gas was released. It didn't stop the others. They were still tearing down Communist flags and ripping off their stars, while still flying their Hungarian flags.

The government fought back, then the next thing everybody knew, Soviet tanks were rumbling through Budapest. Soviet soldiers were continuing to shoot at the crowds and the crowds were shooting back. People were throwing Molotov cocktails in the streets and burning their Communist books. It was pure madness. The trams stopped running and all of the stores and factories closed.

At one point, crowds started to attack the government buildings, causing our Prime Minister to flee. It was then that Imre Nagy actually took over as Prime Minister, just as The Sixteen Points had demanded. He called for peace and tried to call off the violence.

A few days later, he announced Hungary's withdraw from the Warsaw Pact, which had been the ultimate symbol of Soviet dominance, and appealed for status as a neutral state. He even released Catholic Cardinal József Mindszenty from prison.

We were ecstatic. *Could it be?! Could this really be happening?*

Our new government then agreed to open the western border to Austria. The order was issued to take down the barge wires and the search light towers, which had been referred to as The Iron Curtain.

Finally! It's real! We are free!

But our freedom was not to come that easily.

Communist symbol cut from our flag

THIRTEEN

The Ten Second Miracle

At dawn on November 4, I woke up in terror hearing explosions all over the city. We turned on the radio to hear our leader, Imre Nagy, requesting assistance from the rest of the world: the Soviet Union was re-occupying our country with force. They weren't giving up Hungary without a fight. We wondered if our withdrawing from the Warsaw Pact, which is what gave them control over us, had put them over the edge.

After a few days of courageous fighting by our young, unprepared, and poorly-equipped soldiers and civilians, we were not able to resist the mighty 150,000 new Russian troops and their thousands of well-built tanks. The Russian army easily took us over. Not one nation came to our aid. The Russians consequently arrested Nagy and executed him, throwing him in an unmarked grave.

Just when we were so close to freedom, it had all been taken away. We were crestfallen. We saw very little hope for our future and spent the next few days being depressed. Thousands of Hungarians were arrested or deported, some even executed. As for my brave college friends? I never saw them again. I never knew what became of them, but inside I saluted them for most likely giving their lives to fight the tyranny of Communism with their bare hands. I told myself that whoever died during that fight did not die in vain; their spirits would live in my memory forever.

Within days, a new prime minister was in charge. His name was Kádár János (formerly under Nagy as Minister of State) and many felt he was under pressure from the Soviet Union, caving to their demands. He was a little more merciful, but still we were back under the Communist regime. The city stayed full of Russian army tanks patrolling the streets.

I was coming home from school one day and saw a long line formed in front of a little market close to our home. My mother had told me that any time I saw a line for food, it didn't matter for what, to get in line and stay there. She gave me some money to use in such a case, so I was prepared that day.

I went and got in the line as my mother had asked. The line went slow and there were maybe twenty people behind me, some who I recognized from school and from the

BUDAPEST, NOVEMBER 1956

neighborhood. I saw two teen brothers who lived on the next street from us as well my mother's friend's daughter (who was eight months pregnant). She had just arrived and was at the end of the line.

Finally, I made it to the front. I got into the store and purchased about two pounds of potatoes, which was as much as they allowed me to buy. When I got out of the store, I glanced toward the east and saw two Russian tanks approaching from the top of the hill. Since there were Russian tanks all over the place at that time to dominate us and keep us in line, I didn't see anything unusual about these two. The revolution was over, they had won, and we knew that there was nothing we could do about it. Nobody fought them anymore.

I said good-bye to some of my acquaintances and started to walk home. I arrived at the corner just past the next building, and just as I turned right onto the street, bullets started spraying everywhere.

I heard the bullets shattering and exploding things, and people screaming. I started to panic. My first thought was, *Oh no, where is my little brother?* He usually walked home from school at that time. *Was he safe? What was happening?* I was in shock. Terrified, I was tempted to look back to see what was happening, but my survival instinct kicked in and I started to run as fast as I could toward home. My heart was beating wildly and I was shaking. *Can I outrun the bullets?* Suddenly it was eerily quiet, but I kept running even though I was out of breath.

I made it home. To my relief, I spotted my brother. He was safely playing with his little friend from next door. I got him in the house fast, locked all the doors, and just waited. I did not understand what had happened, but I knew I didn't want either of us to go outside. A few hours of silence passed, but I was still much too frightened to go outside to investigate. I knew in my heart, deep in my soul, that I had just survived a very dangerous situation. Mama finally came home, and she was just as happy to see us as we were her. She told me what had happened. Everybody standing in line was massacred by that tank full of Russian soldiers with machine guns. All of the innocent, peaceful people behind me waiting to buy potatoes were killed, gunned down in cold blood for no reason at all.

Mama knew I was there and had nearly missed it. She hugged me hard, and we started to cry. We said a long prayer of thanks for my survival, my ten second miracle.

307 BUDAPEST 4023 20/23 0938 =

Nap	Óra, perc	Hivatalos megjegyzések

44843

TÁVIRAT

Vette:

Hívójel	Nap	Óra, perc

Munkahelyszám:

SOPRON 56 X 21 11

Továbbította:

Munkahelyen	Nap	Óra, perc

1026

FOURTEEN

The Telegram

A week after the massacre at the shop, a short and surprising telegram came from my mother's brother. He lived in the United States; Detroit, Michigan, to be exact. It said,

"Be smart and take the opportunity for a better life."

We were surprised the telegram was not censored. We knew what he meant of course; he thought we should leave our country. We had no chance for a decent, free, civilized life with the Communists back in our country. We had some friends who had left the city and we heard they had already made it to Austria.

Could we do the same? It was a big decision.

After some serious family conferences, we made the decision. We needed to take the opportunity to escape to freedom. It was our only hope. We would have to be courageous and take the risk. Life as we knew it at that time was unacceptable. We had to try for better.

Papa said it would be safest if the three of us went first, and as soon as possible. He would stay behind for a few more days to try to sell some of our belongings to raise some money. He didn't want us to be destitute in that big new world.

On November 28, my mother, brother and I took the train heading west and arrived at the last Hungarian train station before the Austrian border. Since we did not have visas to cross the border on the train, we had to get out with several hundred other passengers and continue the additional few miles on foot. That was our only choice. Nobody was allowed to leave the country of the "Workers' Paradise." We had to put our lives in danger in order to try to get out, but in all of our minds, it was worth it.

There was a group of about twenty people, all strangers to us. They gathered around on the platform, asking each other for directions. One man said he knew the route well, so he would help guide us to Free Austria. We followed him.

We were walking all night in the pitch dark. It was a long journey to cross the border. At the darkest hour of the night, just before dawn, the stillness broke. Out of nowhere we were surrounded by machine gun shots and a rocket of bright light.

The sky around us was lit up with an explosion

of bullets. We ducked instinctively, so as not to get hit. We didn't know where to run, we couldn't see. There was a jumble of chaos and shock as I heard screaming, crying, and sobbing, mixed with blasting and the smell of gun powder. Adrenaline and panic rushed through our bodies. We didn't have a Plan B; what would we ***do***?

The Russian soldiers roughly gathered us together in the dark night. I could still hear crying and sobbing, along with footsteps and yelling. *This is it; we will all die any minute. This is the end of our lives.*

About an hour went by, then a large, closed military truck pulled up. We were instructed to get inside, with another captured group. We were smashed in wall-to-wall in the back of that truck, all standing. It was dark and we were treated like cattle. There was dead silence. We were in shock.

Every one of us was at the mercy of the soldiers. We had no way of knowing what was waiting for us. The 100-mile plus journey was pure agony— we all thought we would surely find ourselves in Siberia in a prison camp at the very least. Our minds raced. The truck finally stopped, but we had no way of seeing what was going on. When we got out, we were actually relieved to see that we were in front of an Hungarian jail building. It could have been worse.

The jail must have been under Russian management, because all of the guards were Russian. There were only two Hungarian women working there, taking our information from us. They separated three of us from the group: My mother, my thirteen-year-old brother, and me, then seventeen. They ushered us into a jail cell, but luckily we were together.

We had no way of contacting Papa about our capture. We were considered criminals for trying to leave the country, and we had no rights. A week went by but surprisingly they let us out. It turned out they were short on jail cells, because there were many thousands of people trying to escape being captured.

They promptly took away all of our identification and the little money we had. They told us we could go, but we needed to appear in the People's Court as soon as the date was set. We were to be sentenced for our crime.

It was late afternoon in a strange city, eighty miles from our former home. We did not know a soul. Without any money or identification, we didn't know how we would get back to

Budapest.

After a short walk, somebody tipped us off to go down about a block. There were some Hungarian truck drivers who knew exactly what was happening in the jail and those kind souls waited for the freed people and volunteered to take them to their destinations, if it was on the way of their route. Luckily for us, one of the truck driver's final destination stops was within walking distance from one of my father's distant relatives.

By the time we got to his relatives' apartment, it was very late at night. He was asleep already. He was a kind and decent old gentleman, happily letting us in to spend the rest of the night. He even gave us some money to complete our travel home.

We went home the next day and found Papa

there. We were glad to be home, but we had a huge problem. We were about to face a sentencing that would cost us the little freedom we had left— and maybe even our lives.

By then it was the second week of December and we had heard that the borders were closing up rapidly, as we had found out first hand. The winter set in and it started to snow, which made it an impossible task to attempt another escape. *What were we going to do?*

We decided we had no other choice. In any way possible, we must try to get to Free Austria. It was a matter of life and maybe death. The biggest issue was that the government by then did not allow anybody to board trains to get to the border town. Even if they did allow it, we had no identification. It would be impossible to travel anywhere. How would we find a way to get 180 miles to the border? Nobody we knew even had a car.

It took Papa several weeks to search, secretly. Luck was with us, but it would cost us all of our worldly possessions. Papa found a reliable man who worked for the railroad. He knew the route and was willing to help us escape. It was a very serious situation, one that could land both him and us in a work camp, in jail, or dead. We felt lucky to have found this man and gave him everything we owned as payment for his help.

It was January 7, 1957, when he was finally able to help us. Everything had to be planned carefully. We had to travel in the dark of night again, this time with Papa. The man was able to put all four of us in a freight train at a remote location. He unlocked the door of one of the containers and we entered it. It was pitch dark inside and there were lots of smelly wood crates and no windows. We found some boxes to sit on while the man locked the doors and instructed us not to make any noise, especially when the train stopped. Then he left us.

Luckily, the train stopped only once. It took several hours to reach the border town, but it felt much longer because we were exhausted, fatigued, cold, and terrified someone would find us. When it stopped again, we heard somebody opening the lock.

We held our breath.

We were relieved to see that it was our man.

"We are close to the border," he said.

We got out of the train; it was dusk by that time. He took us to a nearby warehouse and instructed us to wait for him again. We ate some sandwiches we had packed for the journey.

The man came back when it got dark again and informed us that the coast was clear, and that a young couple with an infant would be joining us. He didn't offer any explanations. We were not happy about having a baby come to the secret spot— what if he cried loudly and gave us away? But we had no choice. We were at this man's mercy and were grateful for a chance to escape, baby or no baby.

We left the warehouse in the darkness of the night, and began our long journey through the fields, hoping to make it to Austria and to our freedom on foot.

A few days before we left, there had been a record amount of snow falling, then the weather turned mild and all the snow melted. We considered it a good omen. Now we didn't have to worry about being spotted on the snowy field. But it brought us another problem. The ground had become very muddy and soft, and it was a struggle to lift our mud-caked shoes out of the boggy ground. The man was annoyed with us. He had a uniform and boots on so his shoes weren't getting stuck in the mud like ours were. Finally, the mud won. It became impossible to walk with our shoes on. They were holding us down like weights. We decided to walk in our stocking-covered feet. We carried our soaked and heavily mud-covered shoes, which felt impossible.

By then, the search towers of The Iron Curtain were back in operation and we knew that their powerful search lights would be sweeping the area for escapees. A large light started shining our way and we knew we needed to avoid it at any and all costs. The only choice we had was to lie on the ground and be completely still when the search light reached us. It was absolutely terrifying to think we had come that far and could possibly be caught. We laid there in the mud, holding our breath, hoping the baby wouldn't cry.

Please don't let us get caught.

Please...

REFUGEES ON THEIR WAY TO AUSTRIA. THEY WERE THE LUCKY ONES; THEY COULD WALK THROUGH THE BORDER IN PEACE. A FEW WEEKS LATER, THE RUSSIAN SOLDIERS TOOK OVER THE BORDER'S SECURITY AND THE WATCH TOWERS

FIFTEEN

Free Austria

The search lights passed over us. We were safe.

We walked for several more hours until we finally reached a road. Our feet were killing us and we were out of breath, dog-tired, and ready to drop. We immediately spotted a German sign.

The man said we were there. We had made it.

Papa collapsed from anxiety and exhaustion. The man wished us goodbye and best of luck, then went back to take possession of all our belongings. He deserved them.

We were cold and barefooted but gloriously free. I cried with absolutely joy and gratefulness, tears breaking through the dirt on my face. We thanked God for our safe journey. He had been with us the whole time. The baby hadn't even cried. It was 3 a.m. by the time Papa got his energy together and got up. Unexpectedly, we saw the light of a vehicle approaching us from far away. Soon a car arrived and stopped in front of us. A woman inside asked us in German, "Are you refugees?"

Mama, in fluent German, said, "Yes, we are."

They motioned for us to get in the car. Mama told them we were full of mud, but they did not care. They drove us to the nearest town. We thanked them a million times for their kindness and told them we had no money to pay them, but they said they were just happy we had made it and that we were there and free. They took us to a barn, which was set up with food and hay on the ground on which to sleep.

We later found out those kind Austrian souls volunteered in shifts to drive out to the country roads in all hours of the night and day just to help the refugees.

We were exhausted and fell straight asleep on the hay. In the morning, a new group of refugees arrived.

People brought us breakfast and a big box of used shoes. We were so thankful and overwhelmed by their kindness. A small bus arrived and a few men got out. They took our information and told us they were there to transport us to a refugee camp.

They took us to a place called Camp Judenau, located in Niederösterreich, Austria. It was a converted boarding school, about forty miles outside of Vienna, and it held close to 800 refugees. The Austrian Red Cross had organized the camp and student/church volunteers helped to run it. The people of Austria donated clothing and blankets and many of them helped to organize the assistance. There was such a large number of people escaping Hungary that Austria asked for assistance from several governments to fund the emergency situation. We had to share a room with hundreds of people sleeping in bunk beds, but we were at peace, so we did not mind. There was hope and freedom in our future.

We signed up to relocate to the United States, but until that could happen, we were to stay in the refugee work camp. Austria was wonderful, and we were very grateful for its citizens' kindness and hospitality. We worked only for our own keep. I was privileged enough to teach the first and second graders to read and write. Under the circumstances, we had no chance to earn any money in the camp, and getting an outside job wasn't feasible due to the unknown time of our departure to the U.S. We were constantly on standby to receive our visas. It could have taken days, but in the end we waited almost a year to receive them.

During this time, somebody gave me an English textbook. I tried to master the language in order to prepare myself for my new home, but there was nobody there to teach me the proper pronunciations, so it was difficult.

I was taking a walk in the city one afternoon, as I always did, when I turned around to go back to my camp. By chance or by design, I will never know, a tall man stepped out in front of me and greeted me with a big smile. I froze. Immediately I recognized him.

Comrade Isti.

My heart sank to my feet. *No. No.*

"What are you doing here?" I asked, terror-stricken.

"I saw the problem with Communism," he said. "When the revolution broke out, I went to the Freedom Fighters' side and fought with them. I was wounded, and they took me to the forest of Bakony. Finally, I healed and just now I was able to escape."

His speech was fast and not believable, especially because by then the border was completely closed, heavily secured, and guarded. It didn't ring true to me.

"I understand," I said with caution. "I am glad you are all right and free."

I wanted to finish the conversation as quickly as possible, and get away from him.

"Sorry, I am in a hurry— I must go," I said.

We said goodbye to each other and I walked away as fast as I could, shaking. I wanted to run, but I tried to behave as if everything were normal.

Was what he said true? I asked myself. *How can anybody who was so entrenched in Communism turn against it that quickly? Was it possible?*

The next day there was a large bulletin pinned to the camp news board:

IMPORTANT! BE CAREFUL! THERE IS A SPY AMONG US. TWO NEW INCIDENTS OF KIDNAPPING REPORTED WITHIN LAST TWO

DAYS.

It couldn't be him...could it?

The following day, a new bulletin appeared. They had caught the spy who was responsible for the kidnapping. It was not Comrade Isti; it was a young father who I frequently saw walking with his wife and two little toddlers. He was well-trusted and even employed to do some administrative job in the camp. Nobody suspected him. He was an intellectual, very vocal against communism, and seemed to be a nice, decent family man. We were all surprised, but it was the same old story: *We still can't trust anybody.*

The next day I took my usual route walking to the town when I happened to walk casually by a small restaurant and looked toward the door.

Comrade Isti was inside, sitting at the very rear table with the wife of the captured spy.

He had not changed. He was no Freedom Fighter. He was at the camp as a spy and for all I knew he could kidnap us.

I ran home as fast as I could.

I was trembling. *I am in big danger. I am not free. He is here to take me back.*

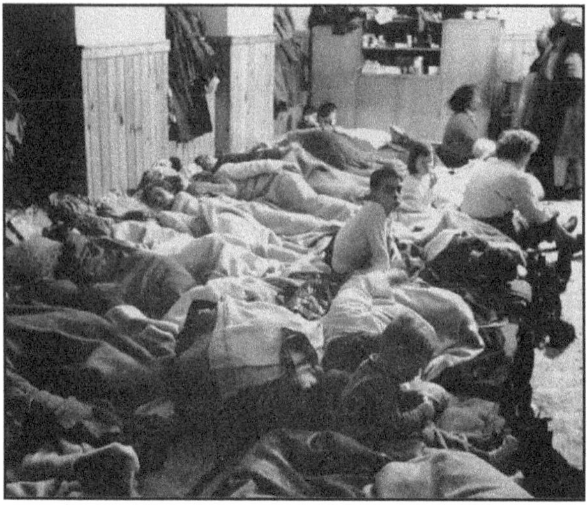

Hungarian Refugees in Austria

SIXTEEN

Panic

The sudden reappearance of Comrade Isti sent me into absolute terror and panic. Had our escape been in vain? This vicious Communist man had found me again, and he could kidnap me. He could take me back, and I could lose my freedom with one wrong move.

Mama and Papa came into our room and found me sobbing. We had been residing in the camp for ten months by then, and being a family of four, we were lucky enough to earn the privilege of having a private room during those last few months. I told them what I had seen. They hugged me, and told me everything was fine, but I saw on their faces that they were worried. What could we do? Going to the authorities of the camp was too risky. We didn't know what to think. Was he connected with the people in the camp? Was the whole thing a trap, filled with spies? Who could we trust? *No one*, we decided. We thought it would be safer to not mention him whatsoever. Luckily, we had already received our immigration papers, so the only thing we were waiting for was our airline tickets to New York. We just had to be very careful within the next few days. We were so *close.*

Papa put one of the beds in front of the door at night, barricading it. I could not sleep those nights. As soon as I dozed off the nightmares came: I was back in Hungary, trying to escape over and over again.

A few agonizing days went by, but I never left

the room. Papa went down to collect our food and mail, but the airline tickets were slow to arrive.

A whole week went by like this, until one morning Papa walked in with the mail and a great smile. He had the tickets to our freedom.

There were two envelopes, one with official airline tickets and one small blue envelope. The small blue envelope was addressed to me with no return address on it. I thought nothing of this; I frequently got mail. I had made lots of friends through the months staying in the camp. When one of them immigrated to another country they often wrote me letters, telling me about their new home. But this blue envelope was not from any other country, it had been mailed locally. *That is odd*, I thought. I opened it and started to read:

Dear Györgyi,

It is so lonely in the world without any family and friends, and since I know you from home to be decent girl, I would like to ask you to be my wife.

Isti B.

I screamed. What the heck was ***this***? He had hated me, the great-granddaughter of the aristocrats! He had intimidated and terrorized me, holding the information on my relatives over my head, making me think that one wrong move on my part would cause my family and me imprisonment or death.

Mama read the letter. She said nobody would ask someone to marry them in such a manner. It just rang false. She had a bad feeling about it. Her instinct was that it was a ploy, a serious ploy. She was convinced: Isti really wanted to kidnap me. She said he was probably looking for me over the past few days and couldn't find me. This was the way to get to me. Or so he thought.

"We have to protect you. It is a serious situation," my mother said.

We only had a few days left in that particular camp, then we would leave for another camp near the airport for a final medical examination, and within four days we would be in America.

Would we make it?

Now looking back, it was amazing how our minds were conditioned. Isti still had power over us and was able to harass us in Free Austria, simply because we did not trust the authorities. It was a learned paranoia; the product of many years lived in fear. It was so easy to feel terrorized and intimidated.

The last four days felt like torture. Two days in we got on the bus to go to the other camp. Every person who got on that bus we viewed as an enemy. We were scared someone would prevent us from getting there.

We finally arrived at the other camp. We were not so lucky as to get a private room this time. Instead, we shared a large room with twenty other people. I decided I would not stay in the camp during the day. When we went next door to the hospital for our final medical examination, I spotted a nearly-empty waiting room while walking down the halls. I decided that that was where I would spend my remaining time. Right after breakfast the next day, I went to the hospital and sat in the corner of that waiting room, reading, with my mother's scarf over my head. I wanted to make sure my face was hidden. I trembled at the sight of every new person who entered the waiting room.

Finally, the day of our departure arrived. A special bus came for sixty-five of us. When people were boarding the bus, I examined every single one of them with my learned paranoia.

We all fit in the bus comfortably because nobody really had any luggage. The four of us in my family shared one very small overnight bag and a briefcase for our paperwork. Neither Mama nor I even owned a purse.

It was a very short ride to the airport. Everyone boarded the plane and I sat next to the window. It was such a feeling of relief, such an exciting time. The plane was scheduled to take off at 11:00 am, but there was a problem. It was 11:20 and we were still on the ground. Then the announcement came:

"We are waiting for one more person before we can take off."

The blood froze in my veins. *He found me, and he is coming for me,* I thought. Mama was sitting next to me with her own fears. She was terrified the plane would crash over the ocean, and none of us could swim.

"Mom, he found me. I know he did," I whispered to her.

She tried to reason with me, but she soon turned back to her fears of the plane, of flying, and of impending catastrophe.

My face was glued to the window. I thought about my options for survival if Isti walked onto that plane. What could I do? Where could I run? Where could I hide? Who there could actually save me? I looked around. Everybody was busy talking, nobody paid attention to me.

Everybody was trying to figure out how the seatbelts worked.

One hour of agony went by. Then, from my window, I saw a private car drive up. A small man got out. He was wearing a black coat, a black hat, and had the distinct long grey beard of a rabbi.

"He has finally arrived," someone said. "We will take off in a few minutes now."

The plane door closed behind him, and I quickly said a long prayer, thanking God profusely that I was finally safe. I was so relieved. I promised myself not to put my feet back on European soil until Communism no longer existed there.

After all of that paranoia, we were on our way to the Promised Land. We just hoped that the plane would make it there.

SEVENTEEN

"Is it Real?"

It was a cool, crisp, November day, my little brother's fourteenth birthday. The most memorable, special day in my life, full of hope and wonders. Was this the beginning of the best of times? The small commuter bus stopped next to the curb of a very busy street in Times Square, New York. The year was 1957.

"Welcome to your new country," our guide said, with a broken Hungarian accent. "We will let you out here to have a chance to look around, and to enjoy the city. You will have three hours to look until we pick you up again right here in front of this restaurant. This is the heart of the city, but do not go too far, it is easy to get lost here. Make sure you can see this advertisement at all times," he said as he pointed to a huge electronic moving billboard. "That will give you good direction. We will come back to take you to the airport. You will have plenty of time to catch your flight to Detroit, Michigan."

The streets were unbelievably busy. People were walking from all directions, and there was very heavy traffic of autos, taxis, and buses. Lights were flashing everywhere.

Is it real...or just a dream? How could this miracle happen to us, so unexpectedly, so fast?

I took a deep breath. *So this is what freedom feels like? Looks like? Smells like?*

There were so many emotions to deal with at one time. We were very tired and overwhelmed, yet relieved and excited.

We had a good night's sleep the night before. It was our first night in the United States and we had stayed at the Hotel St. George in Brooklyn. It was easy to fall asleep in a comfortable bed after thirty-six hours of air travel from Vienna to New York.

We had traveled in an original World War II military plane converted to a passenger plane. The old bird was used up and tired— it frequently needed refueling and long rest times.

We had left Vienna two hours later than originally scheduled. Our first stop was Ireland, to refuel. It was dark when we arrived and it was several hours until we took off again.

It had been very cold in the plane, the seats were uncomfortable, and the noise of the engine was so loud we couldn't have a conversation with the person next to us. There was constant turbulence, but the passengers showed very little of their fears. Most of them prayed in silence, sometimes counting their blessings out loud. The most important thing for us sixty-five passengers was that we were finally free. We were out of the clutches of the Russians and the Hungarian Communist tyrants.

I remember looking out the window and seeing the sun's rays on the horizon. It was the promise of a new day, the promise of new hope. A few hours later, we arrived at our next stop: Reykjavik, Iceland.

Though the sun was still on the horizon, it never fully rose. That was Iceland in November. The plane circled over the city a few times before landing safely. After a few hours of rest, we took off again, excited. Our next stop was supposed to be New York, but the pilot informed us that the plane needed servicing. We landed again in the dark late evening. We were in Newfoundland, Canada, and spent a very long, cold night there.

Some people started to complain, but soon stopped when they were reminded by fellow passengers how very lucky they were, compared to the millions of European immigrants before us, who had to make their journey in boats. It took them weeks to reach their destiny. Thousands of Hungarians had been arrested, imprisoned and tortured. Many had died of starvation and of foul conditions after being forced from their homes and made to live in camps. Some were executed. We were the lucky ones.

The plane took off again at sunrise and we were all relieved and excited. We would be in New York in a few hours, in our new home: The spacious, abundant, good old free America.

Then our pilot melodically announced over the intercom in English, "We are approaching New York, U.S.A., your new home," and it was shortly repeated by someone in Hungarian so we could all understand. Everyone clapped. There were all kinds of emotions present. There were tears of joy, the feeling of being overwhelmed and afraid of the unknown. But we all knew in our heart that our future was to be much better than what we left behind.

The plane circled over New York City for two hours, because we were late and needed permission to land, as they explained to us. As far as I was concerned, the delay was God's gift to us. It was a pure delight, a sight I will never forget. The view was unbelievable: The skyscrapers of Manhattan, the Hudson River, and the harbors. Then the majesty of the Statue of Liberty appeared. I will never ever forget the first time I saw the Lady, the symbol of freedom, from high in the clouds. I had seen pictures of her in Vienna and a few grainy images in newsreels at the movies. They were nothing compared to seeing her in real life. Even at my tender young age, I somehow knew this was the special symbol of my salvation, and it represented my love for my new country. Even when I see it now, decades later, it still brings tears to my eyes. It always brings the feeling of gratitude, the feeling of privilege and joy. It still symbolizes freedom and what this country has provided for me.

Freedom, as we sixty-five passengers knew that day, was the most important gift an organized society could give its citizens. As with so many other things in life, one did not value it as much, until it was lost. Freedom was everything, since we knew life without it.

EISENHOWER ELNÖK LEVELE MAGYAR FORDITÁSBAN

Magyarországról érkezett barátaim:

Amerikai honfitársaim nevében üdvözlöm Önöket az Egyesült Allamokban.

A körülmények, amelyek között elhagyták hazájukat és szeretteiket és mindaz, amit elviselnek, mély megindultsággal és együttérzéssel tölti el az amerikai sziveket. Mélységes és felelösségteljes büszkeség tölt el bennünket, hogy a szükség idején hozzánk jöttek.

A magyar nép századokon át bátran ellenállt az elnyomásnak. Bátor szelleme ma továbbra is mindenütt megihleti a szabad népeket.

Amerikai örökségünk, hogy egyéni szabadságunkat érvényesitsük és más népeknek, amelyek szabadságukért küzdenek, mintahogy mi küzdöttünk egykor, olyan támogatást és menedéket nyujtsunk, amilyet csak tudunk.

Magánpolgáraink közül sokan és az Egyesült Államokban müködö önkéntes szervezetek csatlakoztak kormány-hivatalinkhoz, hogy Önök segitségére lehessünk, hogy Amerikában uj életet teremthessenek.

Hazánk és törvényeink eleinte talán idegenszerüek lesznek az Önök számára. Lehetséges, hogy néhány szükséges eljárás, amelynek utján életünkbe belekapcsolodnak, kisebb kényelmetlenségekkel jár. De arra kérem Önöket, mindig gondoljanak arra, hogy a formálitások mögött mi lakozik amerikai sziveinkben—öszinte óhaj, hogy megszoritsuk a kezüket, hogy kölcsönösen megértsük egymást és hogy igaz barátok és szomszédok legyünk.

Igy üdvözöljük Önöket Amerika földjén. Tudjuk, hogy bensöségesen reménykednek annak az idönek az eljövetelében, amikor minden magyar magyarországi szülöhazájában élvezheti az egyéni szabadság áldásait. Mi is együtt reménykedünk Önökkel. És biztositjuk most Önöket arról, hogy ha ez a nap ismét felvirrad és vissza akarnak térni szülöházájukba, Amerika mindent el fog követni, hogy segitse Önöket visszatérésükben.

Dwight D. Eisenhower

Our Welcome Letter to the U.S.

EIGHTEEN

The Big Apple

Eventually, our plane did arrive in New York City, and our relief was unimaginable. The first order of business was to go to the immigration offices and become legal citizens. The people at the office asked us if we wanted to change our names to English names. We decided to keep our last name as it was, but change our first names. My father Erno became Ernest. My mother Zsuzsanna became Susanna. My brother Laszlo became Leslie. And though my Hungarian name had been Györgyi since the first grade, I had been christened "Georgetta" on my birth certificate in Hungary, so we kept my name.

With our new names, we were ready for new and exciting challenges. They had taken us from Brooklyn to Manhattan, the hub of New York.

My first impression of New York City was that it was a sensational, absolutely amazing place. While Budapest and Vienna were old historic cities, full of impressive buildings (even though most of them had been partially destroyed), New York, on the other hand, was as the name implied. It was fairly new and full of innovation and energy. It was in a free country where people could build bigger, better, taller structures in a much shorter time. It was truly astonishing to people like us. Everything one could want and need for a good life was right there on that small island of Manhattan.

The United States was a picture of booming capitalism at that time. The war was over, the baby boom was in progress, and the growth of the economy was the most vigorous it had been in years. It was an extraordinary period of industrialism and it seemed the whole place was a pinnacle of optimism and prosperity.

The volume and the variety of goods in New York was breathtaking. We were flabbergasted by not only the abundance, but also the affordable prices. There were stacks of gorgeous clothing to the ceilings in some stores, and rows upon rows of shoes in others. We were so used to standing in long lines for food, and many times not even getting it or not being able to afford it. To see a place with so much and so many types of food, lined up in rows and rows, every color, shining, glistening at us, was blissful. Shelves upon shelves of products in bright packaging; toys, electronics, books, everything a person could dream of, were there for purchase, if one so desired. No one told the people of New York what they could and couldn't buy. It was their decision, theirs and theirs alone. They could read books of their choice, listen to music of their choice, and go where they pleased, without answering to anyone. It was nothing short of amazing.

The first store we spotted was a camera store with hundreds of cameras on display. As I looked at them, I thought back to Hungary. We didn't own a camera, but Mama had wanted pictures of us. She once asked her boss if he would take pictures of her children if she provided the film. He agreed, so Mama saved a week's pay for a roll of film, enough to take twelve pictures. When she finally gave him the roll of film, he was so excited to have it that he used most of the shots on his own children. We only got three shots, and those were the only pictures I have of my Communist childhood.

My brother was in even worse shape; because I'd been born before the war, my parents had been able to take photos of me as a baby and small child, before film became scarce. But he had exactly one picture of himself between birth and age fourteen. That was Communism for you.

Papa saw a basic camera for $2.99 there in New York. We thought, *Could this be true?* It most certainly was. We knew the minimum wage at the time was a $1.00 per hour. *One can buy a basic camera for three hours of work?*

When we got hungry, we chose a wonderful street food vendor selling hot dogs. We bought six of them, and four Coca-Colas. The total came to $1.30! It was unreal to us that we could buy a modest dinner for four with the minimum wage of a little over one hour's worth of work. At that moment, we knew we no longer had to worry. We would make it in our new country. We looked at each other and started to weep, counting our fortune of $40 that was sent to us by my mother's brother. He also paid for our New York to Detroit plane tickets.

We still had sadness remembering the friends we had left, who were forced to live a miserable existence. But our gratitude for our own situation was overwhelming. People may not have understood how happy we were just to be there in the United States. People may have thought it was irrational and foolishly optimistic. We were in a foreign country with only $40 and we didn't even know the language. But there was no greater happiness than freedom. There was nothing better than the hope and the possibility of achieving one's dream. There was nothing more elating than the thought that we could become everything we were meant to be.

NINETEEN

Land of the Free

Three hours went by in New York on that first day, and then we met our immigration contact back at the appointed meeting place.

After a short wait, the commuter van arrived. We got in, and the vehicle pulled out slowly into the heavy traffic. We were on our way, traveling toward our unknown future.

We got back to the airport promptly. Our Hungarian guide came with us and made sure we boarded the right plane at the right time. We were very thankful for his service. It was not easy to travel when we didn't speak the language. We felt helpless, almost infantile. He wished us lots of luck and left us as we boarded the plane.

Now we were completely on our own. We were hoping that the schedule was accurate and that we would have our loving uncle and his family waiting for us when we arrived in Detroit. It was late in the evening by that time, but the flight was only going to be about an hour.

My mother was thirsty, and after having studied English for about a month by then, I was sure I could remedy this for her. I had practiced the phrase, "May I have a glass of water?" repeatedly, and by that time I was very confident in my skill. I motioned to the stewardess, and she promptly came over and asked if we needed anything. I very carefully said my first English sentence out loud to another person. I was so proud of myself.

To my surprise, she did not understand what I said. I could see by her face that she had no clue what I was trying to say. She asked me to repeat it, and I did, but even after a few tries, I still could not communicate what I needed. Finally, I just showed her, pretending to drink from a cup.

"Oh," she said, "You want *water*."

When she said the word, it sounded so much different from the way I was saying it. In Hungarian, we wrote very phonetically, and everything seemed to be pronounced exactly the way it was written, but that was not the case in English, I realized. That was my first painful lesson of the English language, and I became scared that it was going to be much harder to learn the language than I thought.

It was past 10 p.m. by the time the plane landed

in Detroit. We were all very emotional and anxious, looking forward to meeting up with our relatives, who we hadn't seen in many years. I hadn't seen my cousin Olivia since we were toddlers, and now we were nearly eighteen years old, almost grown-ups. It had been sixteen years.

The plane stopped on the tarmac, and we followed the line of passengers to get out. We went down a long staircase into the dark, chilly air. Even though there was a crowd of people, we knew who our family was right away. We had a tearful and joyous reunion; we were so indebted to them for bringing us there. We were so grateful.

We walked in the freezing cold to the poorly-lit parking lot and saw that they were getting into two different cars, because there were four of them and four of us.

"You have *two* cars?" My mother couldn't believe it. My uncle laughed and said that of course they had two cars- it was America, after all. The cars were older models, but we couldn't tell the difference. We were just amazed, as we did not know anybody personally who owned a single automobile in Europe, let alone knew how to drive one. Some people in Vienna had their own small European cars, but most people zipped around on colorful mopeds.

My uncle drove one car and my cousin Olivia, who was my age, drove the other. I thought it was astonishing. I couldn't believe someone so young could maneuver that large American vehicle.

After a short trip, we arrived at their home. We could not stop hugging each other. *Finally, I have relatives again*, I thought.

My uncle, who was an engineer, had formerly lived in Vienna. He had lived through most of the bombing just outside of the city during World War II. When the war ended, he was not eligible to stay in Austria. He went to bombed-out, defeated Germany, where many workers were needed to put the country back together. Because he was considered a "displaced person," which meant someone who had been forced to migrate, he had the chance to apply for a green card and immigrate to the United States. In the late 40's he was granted the green card, and he came and got a job at the most famous automobile manufacturing company in the world at that time: Ford Motor Company in Detroit.

My uncle now owned a two-story brick building, which had store spaces that he rented out downstairs. He and his family lived in the comfortable flat upstairs, complete with a large kitchen, built-in cabinets, an electric stove, ovens, and refrigerator. We were centuries behind in Hungary. We had never seen a refrigerator, let alone one filled with food. We couldn't believe our relatives had a washer and a dryer. We were in awe of all of the modern appliances, none of which had been available to us in Hungary, even though it was already the late fifties by then. They also owned a television, which I had never seen. It seemed unreal that a person could have all of this in their home, along with their freedom. My uncle had lived in the U.S. not even ten years, and had accumulated all of that? Not even speaking the language?

"This is a miracle," we told him.

"Yes, I know this looks like a miracle to you—and that is why I sent you the telegram. I didn't

Aunt Sonya, Olivia, Johnny and Uncle John

want to describe this life in detail because I knew it could be censored and you could get in trouble. I felt terrible for you and wanted you to come here."

We went to sleep that night with smiles on our faces. I woke up very early, when it was still dark outside. It must have been around 5 a.m. It took a second to figure out exactly where I was.

The house was quiet; everybody was still asleep. I looked over to my cousin's bed. I couldn't see her in the dark, but I could hear her breathing. She was sound asleep.

It is real. I am here.

Later that morning, I smelled fresh brewing coffee and heard bacon sizzling. My aunt was busy in the kitchen making us breakfast. I dressed quickly so I could give her a hand in the kitchen, but my mother got there first. We were so thankful for their hospitality that we did not want to burden them with extra work.

There was fresh fruit, eggs, bacon, rolls, coffee, milk, and orange juice on the table. So much food for one breakfast? On a lucky day in Hungary, my mother could fry us an egg or two. But my usual breakfast was milk and a piece of bread, if we could get it.

"All of this food," my mother said, looking at the table.

"We appreciate your hospitality, but we definitely do not want you to spend so much money on us," she said. It looked like they had spent a half of a week's salary on just that one breakfast. They assured us it was nothing; buying food was a very small part of their income, not to worry.

We ate and cleaned the kitchen, and then my aunt asked me if I would like to accompany her to the supermarket.

Supermarket?

We had markets in Hungary, but I had never heard of a supermarket. There was one central market in Budapest where the collectives brought their produce from the farms, but it was usually closed in the wintertime, because by then nothing was growing. We put our coats on, and I saw Olivia looking at my faded, olive green army coat. She asked about it, so I told her the story of it— how it had been my uncle's military coat, how my aunt had saved it for twenty years.

"Wow, it kind of looks it," she said.

I didn't know what she meant by that, but judging by the look on her face, she was not impressed with my wonderful, secondhand army coat.

My aunt was ready, and off we went to the American supermarket. When we arrived, my jaw dropped. Rows upon rows upon rows of beautifully packaged food items in a huge store. I'd had a taste of this variety in New York, but this was even better.

I saw forty different types of bread. Marbled rye,

pumpernickel loaves, sourdough baguettes, twisted challah bread, sliced wheat bread, delicate croissants, and round English muffins. I saw the longest meat counter I had ever seen, full of different cuts of meat— legs of lamb, thick steaks, whole chickens, dozens of different sliced deli meats, pork chops, sliced bacon, and hamburger meat. I had never seen so much meat. I couldn't stop staring.

When we got to the produce section, I was completely dumbfounded. Despite it being a snowy November, there was a huge amount of fruit and vegetables inside that store. Pyramids of bright oranges, green grape bunches, red shiny apples, round heads of lettuce, clusters of carrots, green peppers, and hundreds of other beautiful, fresh items and spices. Our winter food, which my mother painstakingly saved for many months when it was available, consisted of cabbage, onions, and potatoes if we were lucky. To see all of that variety in the winter was astounding.

My aunt brought her items to the cashier, who filled five brown paper bags.

"Fifteen dollars and forty cents."

Fifteen dollars? Fifteen dollars for all of that food! It would have taken a month of my parents' salary to buy all of that food in our country. I couldn't wait to tell my mother!

We got back home and my cousin Olivia informed me that she had a Yugoslavian friend named Rose who spoke a little Hungarian. She was coming over to take us to some stores.

The doorbell rang a few minutes later, and a pretty girl in a sumptuous beige coat arrived. We exchanged pleasantries and I saw her look at my coat. She was polite, but I saw in her eyes that my coat, just like my cousin's eyes had shown, was not as wonderful as I had thought.

We walked outside to a shiny green four-door Ford car. Rose said it was her brother's car, and since he didn't trust her driving it, he was going to chauffeur us. The car door opened, and I saw a very pleasant-looking young man sitting in the driver's seat.

I got into the backseat and was introduced to Rose's brother. I immediately got the feeling I had known him my entire life. It was an odd feeling, because of course I had never met him before, having grown up in different countries. *Wow, this is strange*, I thought. *I feel like I know this guy.*

I enjoyed looking at the new city, but was slightly disappointed at its lack of beauty— it was not Europe and it was not New York. It was a typical American, blue-collar, factory city, organized and built with utility in mind.

Finally we stopped at a small shopping center with dress shops, and few other stores of that sort. We parked in a large parking lot, which I thought was an interesting concept. *A lot just for cars.*

We got out of the car and went into a small shop with wall-to-wall coats hanging on chrome racks. There were hundreds of different coats in every color: reds, blues, browns and many more. Olivia went to a rack where there must have been a dozen grey coats hanging. She picked up a beautiful grey wool tweed coat with a hood. The whole thing was lined with faux white fur.

"Wow," I said, "it must be warm."

"Do you like it?" she asked.

"Yes...it is gorgeous," I replied.

And it was. It was luxurious and feminine. I had never seen anything like that.

"Try it on," she said.

"Me?"

"Yes— you are my size; I can see it better on you than on me..."

I tried it on. It was wonderfully soft and warm and fitted perfectly.

"Okay," she said, "we'll take it."

"Okay" was a new word for me. I had heard that Americans said that word a lot, but this was the first time I had heard anyone use it.

My cousin picked up a second coat, the same as the first one, and asked the woman to wrap them up. Then she went to the counter, took money from her purse and paid for them. I was puzzled. *Why does she need two of the same coat?*

She looked at me and said, "This coat is my welcome present to you. I loved it so much that I am also buying one for me. It will be nice for us to match."

I was speechless.

"Olivia," I protested, "it is much too expensive of a present. How can you even afford to buy it?" I asked.

"It is easy dear," she smiled. "Don't worry. The two coats are only costing me one week of my salary. I live with my parents, I have very few expenses, and I want to do this for you. I do not want you to run around with that old rag in America."

I burst into tears. My revered old army coat, the one I was lucky to have in Budapest, was a rag in America. But at the same time, her kindness overwhelmed me, and I thought, *Wow, is it possible that I am exchanging my beloved old rag for a brand-new, super elegant coat?! My parents could never even dream of getting me such a thing!*

I could not thank her enough, and my heart was filled with joy. She was so kind to do such a thing for me, to buy me that plush new coat; my first unforgettable present in America.

During the trip back home in the car I held the bag close to me. It still didn't feel real to me because I couldn't help thinking about my meager wardrobe back in Hungary. I thought back to my one school uniform of faded navy blue, made from a very coarse, cheap fabric. I'd had one other dress; it was a sorry-looking, faded red dress with a matching red necktie that Mama found someplace for a very good price. I hated to wear that dress. I avoided school parties just so I didn't have to wear it. I knew my mother had worked hard for it, so I never told her how much I had loathed it. I didn't want to hurt her feelings.

I remembered my mother saving up for a year-and-a-half in order to buy a few yards of special fabric so I could wear a pretty white blouse with a simple navy pencil skirt for graduation. We could not afford to purchase these things ready-made, so she decided she would make the clothes for me, and I could use them when I went out into the working world and got a job. For an entire year, my mother had bought smaller loaves of bread, stopped buying the cheese that normally went with our noodles, (instead using slightly fried breadcrumbs.) We were figuring, after a year and half seriously saving for it, that by that spring we would have enough money to buy the fabric. I felt guilty that the whole family had to sacrifice with a lack of food just so I could have a few yards of fabric on that special day. But none of them complained. Not even my always-hungry twelve-year-old brother. I had a kind family.

Now I looked at my cousin Olivia and her friend, sitting in the front seat of the big, green American car. They were having a pleasant conversation in English. I couldn't hear the individual words— it sounded like one big long blur of sounds. I didn't understand a word, but listened to them anyway.

I thought about how Olivia had graduated just a few months prior to our arrival and had already gotten a job she loved. She was a secretary in a real estate office. I made a mental note to ask her how hard it was to get such a job. A job that paid enough to where you could buy two beautiful coats with a week's pay. America had become really triumphant for me in that minute. Life was being so kind to me. I watched the passing scenery through the windows of the car and I thought, *Now I am free to be what I want to be, what I was meant to be.*

The snowing stopped, and the sun came out from behind the thick clouds. The snowflakes on the trees were sparkling like millions of diamonds welcoming me, celebrating my good fortune.

Olivia turned around in her seat and apologized for not speaking Hungarian.

"To tell you the truth," she said, "It is hard for me to speak— we left Hungary when I was a baby."

"I understand, no need to apologize," I answered. "It would probably help me if you would speak English to me. It might help me learn it faster." I was rather worried about learning English and was nervous that I wouldn't be able to pick it up.

It will work out somehow, I thought. Right at that moment, Rose's pleasant-looking brother turned around from the driver's seat. In broken Hungarian, he said, "I would be more than glad to help you learn it. I have only been here for eighteen months. I was in Germany prior to being here. I understand how it could be difficult to learn English."

I thanked him for his kind offer.

Little did I know that this pleasant new face would be an important part of my assimilation into the American life, but also a part of the rest of my future.

TWENTY

The Classmate

What a relief it was to have those twelve years of misery behind us. We were so grateful to have survived all of the situations we had been in, so grateful to have escaped our country. The worst was over. There was a lot to process, to talk about, to think about, to discuss, but we decided there would be time for that later. Our first priority at that moment was to plan our future.

We sat down and thought about all of our options and what would be the best way to go about them. I mentioned that my brother and I needed to learn English and finish our educations so we could get jobs. I thought those things were of the utmost importance. We needed to do those things in the shortest amount of time possible, so as not to burden our relatives with too long of a stay. We wanted to get on our feet quickly.

The first person we made plans for was my brother. He was fourteen by then and too young to hold a job, so we enrolled him in the neighborhood junior high. The next on the list was me. I still had five months of school left in order to get a high school diploma. I actually had a choice; I could go straight to work or finish those five months. Education was even more important to me after having to fight for it in Hungary. There was no way I wouldn't finish those five months. My parents agreed, and said I could also get a part-time job.

Mama was next. She couldn't get a job as a

preschool teacher, because she didn't speak English. As we went down the list of possible jobs, we saw that her chances were grim. Almost every job required her to speak English, except for cleaning jobs. I thought a cleaning job might be hard on her pride-wise. I was afraid she would feel ashamed to do it. Besides, she wasn't one for housekeeping. She'd had her own housecleaners before the war. But she knew that it was the best option. She said she would get a cleaning job, and that was the end of that.

Our most important item on the agenda was getting a job for Papa. He spoke three languages, but none of them was English. We were worried.

My uncle knew a man at the Hungarian Church who owned a small business resurfacing chrome car bumpers. Since it was a manual job, we thought it could be a good possibility— the man could explain how to do it in Hungarian, and my father wouldn't have to speak English. That coming Sunday, after church, we met the man and he agreed to hire my father. Soon thereafter, my mother got a cleaning job, and I got a job vacuuming the church rectory. It was a good start for us.

My uncle took me to the closest high school, but they would not enroll me. They told me I needed to go to a special high school, one designed for foreign students. Northern High School was twenty-five miles away, but it was doable. I would simply have to take the bus— two buses, in fact. This particular school had an English immersion program, and one subject at a time, they would integrate me into the regular classes.

Having classmates so different from me was a

very interesting experience that I truly enjoyed. I met kids from so many different countries: Greece, Sweden, Germany, Albania, Macedonia, Italy, and Korea. We all struggled to communicate and learn from each other, but it was still hard to learn English. For some reason I picked up a Swedish accent, and for years people thought I was from Sweden. Our teacher encouraged us to watch a lot of television in order to pick up on the language. I remember watching *Popeye* cartoons; it was one of the first things I could understand.

After a month of English immersion classes, I was ready to integrate into the regular classes. I was so excited. Finally I would be with American students. My excitement turned to frustration when I didn't understand much of the lingo and words used by my new classmates, who were from a poor part of Detroit called "the projects." The class laughed at me when I asked what the project was.

I made one girlfriend named Anita, and I felt she would tell me what it meant without laughing at me. She was always raising her hand to answer questions, I knew she must know.

She painstakingly explained to me one day that "the projects," where she lived, were government housing for the "poorest of the poor."

"*You* are poor?" I asked.

I didn't understand. She wore pretty dresses and her father picked her up in a car. How was that poor?

"Trust me, we are poor. That car is very old and my dresses are not pretty at all."

"Well you could have fooled me," I said in the best English I could. "Your dresses are more beautiful than any elegant woman's in Budapest."

She smiled and said, "If you say so."

"We don't even have a car," I said. "We are poorer than you are."

She smiled sympathetically.

"Can I go to see your project sometime?" I asked naively.

"Sure," she said. She never became insulted by my ignorance; she was very kind about it.

One day I walked home with Anita. We stopped in front of a large apartment complex. It was a little shabby, not kept up very well. It wasn't grand, but it wasn't partially bombed or falling apart, either.

When I walked through Anita's front door the first thing I saw was a television in the room. Then I looked over at one of the end tables and saw a telephone. We walked into the kitchen to put our books on the table and I saw a lovely, large gas stove, and a large refrigerator.

Wow.

That day solidified another reason for my love of the United States: the "poorest of the poor" lived better than the privileged few in Hungary. I knew right then it was true: You could learn a lot about a nation by the way it treated its lower class.

OUR FIRST HOME IN THE U.S.

TWENTY-ONE

A New Home

We lived with our relatives for six weeks and saved every dime we could. People from the church were very helpful in getting out the news of new immigrants, and a lot of people were willing to help us. A Hungarian lady called one day and said she had heard we might need a place to live. She had an opening in her apartment building, and since she knew we were new immigrants, she offered it to us at a very reasonable price.

There was a vacancy in a lower apartment in her duplex. It was located a short distance from the bus stop that my family used. We didn't have a car, and none of us yet knew how to drive. We did have enough money to pay the first month's rent and a half a month's security deposit. People in the church donated bedding and cooking utensils. We were so grateful to all of them.

During those days, the trend in furniture was mid-century modern: a very sparse, minimalist look of straight lines, made mostly with blond wood. In the face of this new style, many people donated their "outdated" antique furniture to the Salvation Army, where it was sold for next to nothing. Having grown up in an elegant home, my mother had wonderful Old World taste. She scoured the shops and was able to assemble a very fine home for us that would have been absolutely unthinkable to achieve in Budapest.

Someone gave my mother a sewing machine, and within a year I had a dream wardrobe of luxurious, beautifully-crafted clothing. She enjoyed designing my clothes and was a wonderful seamstress.

I earned an extra five dollars one day and my mother told me I could buy whatever I wanted with it. I was so excited. It was the first serious money in my pocket that I had ever had to myself and I could spend it as my heart desired. I remembered seeing a dime store downtown on my bus route, so I decided to go there that Saturday morning.

The store was filled with wonderful goodies. I spent considerable time walking up and down the well-stocked aisles, checking out merchandise and prices. There were so many things that I had to try and narrow it down. I saw a white cotton blouse that looked like the one we had saved for in Hungary. It was only two dollars. I smiled, then put it in my cart. There was a stylish red belt for fifty cents and a pair of black flats, which had been marked down to $1.80 from $5.99. I could not believe my eyes. For five hours of work I could purchase all of these wonderful things and have forty cents left over?! It was a memorable and exhilarating afternoon.

On the way home from the dime store, I thought about school. I had originally wanted to get a scholarship to Oxford, as one of my Hungarian friends had, but I knew that there were good universities in America as well. I just needed to master the language and get that diploma.

My school life was going fine, but my plan to integrate into American society was not. My foreign classmates came and went, so as a result, the cast changed frequently. A set of stunning and polished twin girls came from Sicily, with glamorous hairstyles and fine clothing. I tried to start a conversation with them several times, but they were very short with me, almost secretive, keeping only to themselves. They were picked up in a shiny black Lincoln Town Car every day after school.

One day I mentioned that I liked their father's car, and they said it was not their father but their chauffeur who picked them up. I later found out that their father owned two upscale Italian restaurants on Woodward Boulevard, the most posh street in Detroit. I guessed I was not in their league. I never found out.

The students in the foreign class lived in all parts of the city, some near, some far, and none really on the same route, which prevented us from getting together socially. There was one girl I did ride the bus with frequently, a Macedonian girl named Betsy. She was real cute with her pixie haircut, poodle skirts, and bright red lipstick. She told me her family belonged to a Macedonian church and she went there weekly for social dances. Her mother bought her a new dancing dress every other week because she wanted her to secure a Macedonian boyfriend. Betsy invited me to go with her, but it wasn't Greek society I wanted to break into, it was American society. I politely declined and stayed friendly with her.

My cousin Olivia's social life also revolved around the church. There was a Hungarian youth club there, and I was frequently invited. It was a mixture of Hungarian people of all ages; some who had been born in the United States, and some who had immigrated with their families to the U.S. at different times throughout the prior two decades. They all had their own story. The old-timers told us endless stories of how lucky we were to come to America at that time, and how hard it had been to live through the Great Depression in the thirties. There was a shabbily-dressed woman named Mrs. Szanto who, even in the midst of winter, wore sandals. She had very interesting stories of her difficult life before immigrating. But the most interesting thing was that despite her disadvantaged background, she had still managed to come to the U.S., becoming the owner of several properties by that time. She owned ten homes, all rented out. One day she approached us. One of the homes had become vacant and she would rent it to us at a considerably discounted rate.

We went to see it, and were pleased to see a very nice, two-story, brick home on a lovely tree-lined street. She only wanted $60 a month for it, barely Papa's weekly salary. Soon we had moved into the comfortable and beautiful private home. It was on the west side of the city, where Ford and General Motors had their offices and some of their production plants.

It was a pleasant area. The streets were attractive and organized, lined with trees. The main boulevard was filled with markets abundant with food, shops stacked with clothes, shoes and toys; pizza parlors wafting with the smell of dinner, and neighborhood drugstores with red stools and soda fountains. All were within walking distance.

I still had to travel to downtown Detroit to go to school. At that time the downtown district was very exclusive and chic; all of the well-dressed ladies shopped there. The seven-story J.L. Hudson on Woodward Boulevard was the crowning glory of the shopping experience, but there were other fashionable department stores lined up next to each other: Saks Fifth Avenue, I.Magnin and others. In my after-school hours, I slowly explored each one of them, along with the rest of the city. There were dazzling boutiques, colorful flower shops, bustling restaurants, picturesque churches, art-filled museums, and the neo-classical Wayne State University buildings.

My social life mostly consisted of spending time with Olivia's Hungarian friends who lived close by. Many of them had cars and could pick us up to go out to dances and what not. We also belonged to the International Institute, a group designed to promote international culture. We Hungarians had our own folk dance group that I happily joined. The irony was that I didn't learn the traditional old Hungarian culture and dances until I got to America. In Budapest, nobody was dancing our most famous folk dance, the Csárdás.

I was still anxious to accelerate my English, so I took an evening class in the neighborhood. There were all types of people in that particular class, many of them from Latin America. There were also a couple of young people living on my block, with who I made friends. They were all relatively busy working or attending college, but sometimes we played tennis together. While I enjoyed the game, it didn't give me much of a chance to converse with them and learn the language any better. I always asked my Hungarian friends to speak to me in English, and though they started out doing so, they would switch back to Hungarian when I had difficulty understanding them.

Watching our snowy, 9-inch black and white

television was one of the main sources of my language education. Whenever my brother and father finished watching what seemed to be hours of cowboys and Indians yelling and running after each other on horseback in the Wild West, I was able to catch *I Love Lucy* and *Father Knows Best*. Slowly, those shows started to make sense to me. I was on my way.

I always wondered if I would have picked up the language faster had I been thrown straight into the neighborhood high school instead of the special school for foreigners. My brother appeared to have picked up quite a bit of English just playing with his American friends in the neighborhood.

I was finally able to finish all my required high school classes, excelling in math. It took three semesters to finish what would've been one semester in Hungary, but I didn't mind. I had to

My High School Graduation Picture, June 1959

My Brother

finish the basic required classes of U.S. History, U.S. Government, English Grammar, and Literature. I was honored to take each and every one. I graduated from high school in the spring of 1959, two years later than I was supposed to. I was in a different country, in a different continent and managed to do it all in a different language. I did it. I was so proud.

It was time to make my future college plans. I would have liked to have been a teacher. I really enjoyed teaching Hungarian children in the refugee camp back in Austria, but my lack of English language capabilities was holding me back. Although they had improved considerably, they were not good enough to be a teacher.

I loved beautiful homes and was passionate about art and design. I think it was in my soul, an inherited part of my DNA. Design was an international language; it did not require extensive English language knowledge, so I chose to study interior design and fine art in college. It was a wonderful choice, and as I found out, it was my lifelong passion.

I deeply appreciated the opportunities I had in the United States to be able to get my education without being harassed. I was free to go to college, free to choose my own vocation, and free to choose what I wanted to learn. I felt very lucky. About a decade afterward, I took a few more years' worth of business classes. I felt truly blessed with the freedom and opportunity to be able to return and continue a college education in later years. I was so grateful to have the opportunities to advance my education, to have a wonderful life, and to create wealth with my passion. I am living proof someone really truly can pursue their own happiness in this country. Someone can truly start from nothing, or in my case, less than nothing.

My Parents

TWENTY-TWO

Return to Budapest

On my first day in the United States, I had met Joe, the pleasant-looking brother of my cousin's friend, Rose. After three years of courtship, Joe became my husband. He had immigrated with his family a few years before we did. He, too, was born in the Transylvanian province of Hungary only fifty miles from where I was born, but his family ended up moving to Germany. His parents saw how dangerous and sad the situation was in Europe, and they opted to immigrate to a safe, dependable, and free United States. Joe's mother's siblings were living in the U.S. They immigrated in the 1910's and settled down in Detroit, Michigan. We may have grown up in different countries, but fate brought us together in America.

After my husband graduated from college in Detroit, we moved to Los Angeles where he got a job. We were happy to live in a great city where we could enjoy beautiful weather all year round. We had three children together, and were so lucky to be able to raise them in a free country, and in a place where the ocean and the mountains were our playgrounds. My parents followed our footsteps and moved to Los Angeles alongside us; together we enjoyed and celebrated our wonderful lives.

We all worked hard, and truly lived the American dream. We had our setbacks, but most of our lives were full of blessings. We had achieved more than we ever dreamed. We were always incredibly grateful and thankful for all of our opportunities and our freedom. This huge country was magic to us. We could live in any city we chose and we were free to travel any place in the world we desired to go. We could read and write whatever we pleased, and we could not only openly express our political views, but we were free to vote for any representative we thought would fulfill our needs. It was a far cry from the oppressed regime we came from. I got my real estate broker's license, and for the next twenty years worked on acquisitions and disposition of commercial properties.

In 1994, I decided it was time to follow my passion of a more creative life, so I got a job as an interior designer.

At the age of 62, I went one step further and opened up my own furniture store, and spent

MY SHOP IN THE NEWSPAPER

the next twelve years running a successful American business.

I am still thankful for the simple things that the American-born may take for granted, like entering a supermarket with an abundance of food and affordable prices all year around. I am so happy to have a wonderful book collection, and to be able to buy new shoes for my children when needed.

I am happy to be able to afford a lovely home filled with things I find beautiful.

By the time my husband and I were approaching our 40th wedding anniversary, we decided we had worked long and hard and it was time to celebrate in style. Our children were grown and gone by this time, having finished college and gone out on their own.

We decided it was time for us to revisit our European roots, since the Berlin Wall had been down over a decade by that time and Communism had disintegrated.

We flew to Germany, rented a car, and started our tour. First we visited the city of Cologne, which is where my husband lived as a young man. Then we drove to Austria to visit the place where my family and I stayed in the refugee camps.

The next country on our agenda was Hungary.

We started our journey very early in the morning, and as soon as we started crossing the border, I felt very uneasy. Vivid memories rushed into my head; reminding me of the last time I had crossed that border so long ago, seeking freedom with my family. My body remembered the fear and the terror; my mind went back to hoping we weren't going to be killed by Russian soldiers, back to crawling in the pitch dark in a muddy field. Even though things were different now and we were decades away from those days, I started to wheeze and I couldn't catch my breath. The anxiety in my body was overwhelming.

We arrived in Budapest in a couple of hours, and had a chance to visit the schools I had attended and the last home my family lived in, which was in shambles by then, the victim of forty-five years of neglect.

We stayed in a new, high-rise hotel in the middle of the city. Joe was especially excited, because it was his first time visiting Budapest. We had a wonderful dinner and we went up to our room to get a good night's rest in order to be fresh for our next day of explorations.

Things did not turn out for us as planned.

I woke up in the middle of the night with a morbid distress. I was absolutely paralyzed and could not breathe. My throat was closing up and I was suffocating, as terrorizing thoughts rushed through my mind. I was sure my life was ending shortly. I remember thinking, *I am not getting out of this city alive.*

My husband was peacefully sleeping in the adjacent bed. I tried to wake him, but I couldn't find my voice. No words would come out of me. Miraculously, I was able to take a small first breath, then a second. Although I was shivering, my muscles started to loosen enough to where I was able to get up and go out onto the small balcony and catch a fresh breath of air. We were on the 11th floor of the hotel overlooking a vast vista of the sleeping city. There were no Russian tanks in sight, no Communists. The demons were in my mind, the memories of terror were of my final day in January of 1957, sitting in my classroom at school, peacefully listening to a lecture. All of a sudden one of my classmates started to scream, as she spotted from the window a line of Russian tanks facing our school, ready to shoot. I remember all of us rushing to the back of the building, and how we had to climb through a large wall to escape to the adjacent hospital.

You are okay. You are okay. It was so long ago, you are an American citizen and this is a free

My High School

country now, I reasoned with myself. It took me a very long time to finally be able to relax. As soon as I did, I saw a light on the horizon. The darkness of night broke and the sun was on its way. A new day was beginning. I was finally able to return to my bed.

That morning, I told my husband what happened. He was very worried about me and thought it would be best to leave. I felt foolish, childish, and terrible. I didn't want to change our plans just because of my feelings of anxiety. I wanted both of us to have an enjoyable time. I suggested we visit the countryside for a few days and then try to come back. We did just that. The problem was, when we returned to the city we drove from the east, visiting the places I lived as a little child during the height of the bombings of World War II. Once again, the memories were unbearable, and I was not able to stay in the city.

That was the only day I have spent in Budapest since then.

Our trip still ended up to be wonderful. We decided to see Italy, the Swiss Alps, and Paris. I love and admire the beauty of Europe: the cathedrals, the museums, the beautiful architecture, all products of the hard work of so many talented people, stretching through hundreds of years of history.

I am proud I was born in Europe. I am just as proud to be an American. There is not as much here to remind one of the histories of the past, but the U.S. has a clean slate and the freedom to build the future. This country is free and a fertile land of innovation, one that has nurtured great inventions and innovations in industry, science, travel and technology. It has really contributed to the advances of the well-being of the world's population— its contribution to the development of humankind are unparalleled. A few good men constructed the Constitution: freedom of speech, a small government, personal rights, property rights and the freedom to pursue one's own happiness. These were some of the important elements, among other things, that have laid the foundation of this country's success. It gave a solid base of laws for a nation to grow and prosper.

We as a family did prosper, and as immigrants and refugees we came to this country with only the clothes on our backs and forty dollars in our pocket, unable to speak a word of English, unable to turn back. We *had* to make it, and we did. With perseverance and hard work, we lived a life of abundance without any outside help. That would have been absolutely impossible to achieve in a socialist, Communist, government-controlled economy.

Life has come full circle as Papa, Mama, my brother and Joe have all passed. Now a new generation has been born into our family, and they are the ones giving my children (including

My Grandchildren

my nephew, Steven, who I consider a third son) and me purpose and joy. We are a truly blessed family, lucky enough to live close to each other, while keeping up our family traditions of getting together frequently to celebrate holidays and milestones.

The new generation is growing, life continues. I

give thanks every day for my four spectacular grandchildren and for the enjoyment of watching them grow and develop. I wrote this book for, and with, my grandchildren in mind.

I hope that by reading this book one day, they will realize how lucky they are to live in freedom. I want to teach them to be grateful to their ancestors for the courage and sacrifice that made such freedom possible.

My wish for them is to know how fragile liberty is, and never to take it for granted, because it can be lost so easily and rapidly. I want to inspire my grandchildren to grow up to have great character and intelligence, and to use these gifts bravely in defense and protection of this country's liberty.

With my Husband

Epilogue

Writing this book was one of the biggest challenges and triumphs in my life.

The process of dealing with my haunting memories and experiences from one of the most tragic times in European history was sometimes just as painful to put on paper as it was to live it. But equally, remembering my triumphs makes me feel just as joyful as the day they occurred. I wrote this book for freedom-loving people everywhere. I hope my story has inspired people to realize how important it is to guard their freedom. How important it is to be a free individual, to be different from everybody else. It is our strength and birthright and should be celebrated. Our uniqueness makes us strong, and the synergy of individuality makes society prosperous.

I also want to express my deepest love for the United States. Millions of people all over the world have done everything in their power to immigrate to the U.S. both legally and illegally. Many more millions are just dreaming of living here. I was one of the blessed immigrants who was admitted to America to pursue my happiness, and I am very grateful for it.

Blessings to the United States and to All,

Georgette Hadvina,

California U.S.A.

MY FAMILY

Acknowledgements

Foremost, I want to express my greatest gratitude to my publisher, Amy O'Hare, at Estep & Fitzgerald. I am forever indebted to her. Without her, none of this book would have happened. I am blessed that I had her guidance, encouragement, and patience.

I also want to express my thanks and love to my dear children: my daughter Cindy, who was a major influence for me to write our family history; my son Eddie, whose support and faith in me never stopped; my son Richard for his patience, kindness and understanding; and my favorite nephew Steven, for all of his encouragement and caring. I would also like to thank all of my amazing nephews and nieces, who have embraced me with their kindness and enthusiasm. I am especially grateful for my four spectacular grandchildren, Jenna, Jack, Erin, and Dana, who make my life a pure joy, and who have inspired me to write in order to leave them a legacy. My gratitude also goes out to my daughter-in-law, Shellie, and my son-in-law, Paul, for being such wonderful, loving members of our family. I have a deep appreciation for my only cousin, Olivia, for her caring and love throughout my life. My many thanks go to all of my dear friends who have encouraged me through the years to document my history.

To my Uncle John I give my utmost gratitude; without him, I would not have had a chance to live a wonderful, free life in the United States. And my very special, deepest gratitude goes to my parents, for their never ending love, even in the harshest, most impossible environment. They taught me the real meaning and importance of family, and what real courage is.

Georgette Hadvina

About the Author

Georgette Hadvina was born as Georgetta Gergely on July 18, 1939, in Petrozseny, once part of the Austro-Hungarian Empire. She was only three years old when the Transylvania province where her family lived was annexed to Romania, causing her Hungarian parents to move to the capital city of Budapest, Hungary. Growing up, she witnessed the destruction of the Second World War, the brutal Russian takeover of the country, the oppression of Communism, and the outbreak and defeat of a revolution. Indulging in her childhood passion, reading was the only way she was able to escape and survive the cruelty of life around her.

After one failed attempt, Georgette and her family were able to succeed in a daring escape to Austria through the infamous Iron Curtain. At eighteen, she immigrated to the United States with her family, arriving as penniless refugees who spoke not a word of English. After learning the language, she graduated with honors from Northern High School in Detroit, Michigan, and went on to study fine art, interior design, and business in college. In the next few decades Georgette successfully pursued several careers -- a commercial real estate broker, an interior designer, and a small business owner. She raised three children with her husband, and was widowed after forty-five years of marriage.

She now lives in Southern California, close to

her family and grandchildren.